DOLPHINS
SEALS
AND
OTHER SEA MAMMALS

COLLINS · Glasgow and London

ANIMAL WORLD SERIES
General Editor
David Stephen

G. P. PUTNAM'S SONS · New York

ACKNOWLEDGEMENTS

Aarons:pp.13(top),22(bottom),25.
G.Bazile:p.13(bottom).C.Belinky:p.49.
G.Bern:pp.29(top),30–31.J.Burton:
p.87(top).Busnel:pp.58–59,64(bottom),
69,70,71.Brosset:p.65(top).J.Cooke:
p.32(top).M.Durrance:pp.76,77.
E.P.S.:p.9.F.Erize:pp.9,10,11(bottom),
15,18–19,22(top),23(bottom),24(top),
34–37,41–43,47,83.F.Bel-G.Vienne:pp.
20,26–27.French polar explorers:pp.13
(bottom),16(top).G.Gerster-Rapho:p.
33.S.Gillsater:pp.11(top),16(bottom),
29(top),30,31,38–39,40,46,61,62,68
(top right).Holmes-Lebel:pp.63,81.H.V.
Irmer:p.48.Jacana:pp.14,20,23(top),
24,26–27,32(bottom),64(top),65(top),
72,75,80,82,88(top).J.Masson:pp.12.13
(bottom).P.A.Milwaukee:pp.64(top),
72(top and bottom),75,80,82,88(top).
Okapia:pp.30(bottom),31,88(top).R.
Peterson:p.45.B.Pierno:p.28(bottom).
Raymond:p.67.Rizzoli archives:p.66.
M.Robert:p.24(bottom).Rouillon:-
Images et Textes:P.21.Russe Kinne-
Photo Researchers:pp.51–57,60,73,
78–79,84–85.J.Six:p.28(top).Dr
Soulaire:pp.65(bottom),68(left),86.
D.Stephen:p.17.B.Tollu:p.23(top).B.
Tulloch-Photo Researchers:p.87
(bottom).J.P.Varin:pp.14,20,26–27,32
(bottom).J. van Warner:p.44.

First published in this edition 1973
Published by William Collins Sons and
Company Limited, Glasgow and London,
and by G. P. Putnam's Sons, New York
© 1968 Rizzoli Editore, Milan
© 1973 English language text
William Collins Sons and Company Limited
Printed in Italy
ISBN 0 00 106106 2 (Collins)
SBN 399 11153 0 (G. P. Putnam's Sons)
Library of Congress Catalog Card Number: 72 98132

INTRODUCTION

Mammals can be quickly and safely defined as warm-blooded animals that suckle their young, have a four-chambered heart, and a covering of hair. Birds, of course, have warm blood and a four-chambered heart, but they do not suckle their young. Nor do they have hair.

Characteristically, mammals are four-legged animals that live on land, and this is the way we tend to think about them. Nevertheless, there are some species well adapted for spending part of their lives in the water. An example is the otter, a land carnivore that can dive and swim and catch prey in water. Another is the beaver, a rodent that can dive and swim, and which constructs its living quarters in water. It is easy to think of others similarly specialized, like the musk rat, the coypu and the water vole—all of them rodents.

There are, however, three large groups of mammals that are fundamentally water mammals. More specifically, they are marine mammals. They move in, seek their food in, and live in the sea. They cannot live away from it. Some of them spend most of their lives in it: others spend their entire lives in it. Whales, for example, die when stranded —when they are beached.

The three groups of marine mammals are the *Pinnipedia* (seals, walruses and their relatives) which live in the water but come ashore to breed: the *Cetacea* (dolphins and whales) and the *Sirenia* (manatees and dugongs) which cannot leave the water at all.

The *Cetacea* and *Sirenia* are well defined orders of the class *Mammalia*. The *Pinnipedia* are usually considered to be a suborder of the order *Carnivora*; that is to say they are carnivores of a special kind. Whether they are special enough to be considered as a full separate order is a question zoologists are still discussing.

Although these three groups—two orders and one suborder—are distinctive and unrelated, they share many similarities. In all of them, the body is sturdy and broadest in the middle. The head is streamlined into the body in such a way that there appears to be no neck, and the tail end is narrow and pointed to a greater or lesser degree. The animals are, therefore, spindle-shaped or fish-shaped. This body shape is an adaptive characteristic, the result of an evolutionary process, or adaptation, that results in unrelated species becoming quite like each other because they lead a similar sort of life. This is the same sort of convergent evolution that can be seen in birds like swifts and swallows which, although unrelated, superficially resemble each other.

Convergent evolution has resulted in marine mammals becoming very like some of the big fishes—for example sharks and tuna fish—because the limbs have become modified into fins or flippers. Because of this, many people still think of dolphins, whales and manatees as fish. But if we examine what lies under the skin—the skeleton and internal organs—we find a mammal, and not a fish.

The skeleton of these marine mammals is that of the land mammals. They have lungs, not gills. Their blood circulation, and all their basic physiology, are typical of mammals, and not at all of fishes. Being mammals, and not fishes, they have to breathe atmospheric air, which means they have to come to the surface regularly for oxygen. They cannot use oxygen dissolved in water, as fishes and frogs do.

Although the presence of hair is one of the characteristics of land mammals, this has become sparse or almost non-existent in many of the marine species. Instead of a fur coat, most marine mammals have developed a thick layer of fatty tissue, or blubber, to insulate them against the cold. Some of the seals have the best of both worlds—blubber and a fur coat.

Marine mammals are usually of considerable size, but this does not hinder them because water offers little friction or resistance to movement. In addition, as the principle of Archimedes shows, the volume of water displaced by an animal reduces its weight. Whales, in particular, prove this point. They are the largest animals now in existence—the blue whale reaches a length of 110 feet and weighs up to 150 tons—but they are agile and active in water, and float as easily as corks. Ashore, they become grounded and die, crushed by their own weight.

Pinnipedia

As already shown, some authorities regard this as a distinct order of the class *Mammalia*, independent of the *Carnivora*. Its evolution has resulted in a fundamental modification of structure adapted to life in the water. The name itself is an illustration of this (*Pinnipedia*: from *pinna*—a flipper, and *pes-pedis*—a foot). The skeleton illustrated in Figure 1 shows quite clearly the presence of fore limbs, hind limbs and feet. But these are hidden in the living animal. The fingers are joined by a strong membrane and show only as claws which vary from species to species.

As can be seen from Figure 1, the hind feet are set far back on the body. They are placed together on the same horizontal plane and propel the animal when swimming, in the same way as a ship's propeller. But they are of little use to it when it is ashore because the greater part of both limbs is enclosed in the body mass. As a result, the animals drag

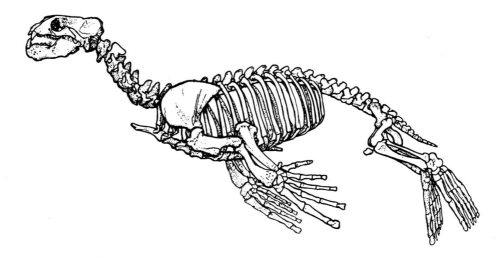

Figure 1: Skeleton of the sea lion. Natural length is seven feet. Note the bones of the fore and hind limbs (the latter placed very far back) with the typical pentadactyl extremity.
After Blainville in P. P. Grassé, Traité de Zoologie.

canine teeth, which are used to hold and tear up prey, are well developed. But the pre-molars and molars are comparatively small. There is not much difference between them, and both are of primitive type. Dentation varies from

incisors	$\dfrac{3}{3}$	incisors		$\dfrac{1}{0}$
canine	$\dfrac{1}{1}$	canine		$\dfrac{1}{1}$
pre-molars	$\dfrac{4}{4}$	to	pre-molars	$\dfrac{3}{3}$
molars	$\dfrac{1}{1}$	molars		$\dfrac{0}{0}$

The bull walrus (see Figure 3) usually has enormous canines protruding well clear of the mouth. This ivory is of great commercial value. The change of teeth from milk to adult has seldom been observed, as the milk teeth are usually lost soon after birth, or are shed while the young animal is still in the womb.

Hair, when it is present at all, is usually short and sparse. But in some species it is thick, compact and lustrous and, consequently, highly valued in the fur trade. The pelts of newly born or very young animals are especially valuable. The possession of a valuable coat is the great misfortune of these animals. Because of it, they have been, and still are, subjected to savage persecution and violent death. They have also been over-hunted and will certainly become extinct unless given protection.

Pinnipeds come ashore to breed, and have their traditional breeding places, or rookeries, to which they return year after year. Breeding stations are on rocky islands and beaches. On the breeding grounds, the males fight fiercely for possession of the females, and it is

themselves about slowly, on land. All the animals in this group are similar in this respect, as can be seen from the illustrations in Figure 2.

It is in this part of their anatomy that seals and whales differ fundamentally. The seals, sea lions and walruses can come ashore to breed, or rest, or sleep, or moult. But the whales, dolphins and sirenians cannot do so. They are exclusively marine, and never voluntarily leave the water. The tail fin of the *Cetacea* is a propulsive organ, but it has no connection whatever with hind limbs, in spite of its somewhat superficial

resemblance to the hind limbs of seals. The external ears of the marine mammals are either very small, or absent. The ear and nose passages can be closed voluntarily when the animal submerges. This is a necessary feature in a diving mammal, and is also found in otters which are similar to seals in this respect. The snout is short. Pinnipeds have a poor sense of smell. Since they close their noses when under water, this is not a great loss.

The eyes of the pinnipeds are well developed and situated on the upper part of the head. The incisor teeth and

Figure 2: The principal species of seals and walruses: 1. Lobodon carcinophagus*; 2.* Monachus albiventris*; 3.* Leptonychotes Weddelli*; 4.* Phoca hispida*; 5.* Phoca Groenlandica*; 6.* Mirounga leonina*; 7.* Cystophora cristata*; 8.* Erignathus barba- tus*; 9.* Hydrurga leptonyx*; 10.* Phoca vitulina*; 11.* Halicorus grypus*; 12.* Zalo- phus Californiaus*; 13.* Phoca fasciata*; 14.* Otaria byronia*; 15.* Calorhinus alas- cana*; 16.* Odobenus rosmarus.
After Kosmos-Lexicon *(ed. Herder).*

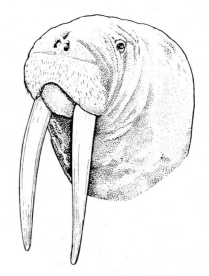

Figure 3: Face of a bull walrus showing the whiskers (tactile hairs on the snout) and the transformation of the huge upper canines into defensive weapons. These tusks can be up to three feet long and weigh 11 pounds. After P. P. Grassé

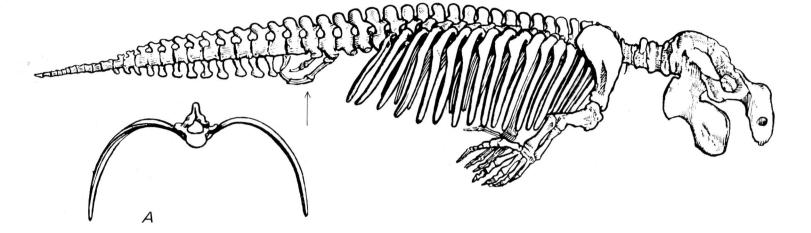

A

not unusual for animals to be severely injured or killed. Mature bulls collect from 30 to 70 females, depending on species. In some species, there is a true harem system. Immature males do not mate, but live in separate groups.

Once the mating season is over, it is quite common to find mixed groups of males, females and young, forming some sort of social organization. Gestation is usually very long, while the suckling period is usually short, from several days to a few weeks; but in some species, it is much longer.

The brains of seals and walruses are well developed. The animals have considerable learning ability, and many species of pinnipeds are well-known and prized as performing animals. The species most commonly found in circuses is the California sea lion which is remarkably docile and learns quickly.

The evolution of the pinnipeds has been well studied. The suborder is now divided into three families: *Otariidae*, *Odobenidae* and *Phocidae*. The black or California sea lion belongs to the first of these families. The giant walrus of the North Pacific belongs to the second. Bulls of this species measure up to 15 feet in length and weigh up to a ton. The gigantic elephant seal belongs to the third group. Males of this species measure up to 20 feet long and weigh up to four tons.

Sirenia

Animals of this group form an order of mammals which, like the whales and dolphins, is totally adapted to a life in the water. They cannot live on land. Sirenians are found in the sea and in river estuaries, and will sometimes penetrate upstream for considerable distances. They are also known as sea cows because of the way in which they graze the sea bottom. They are most closely related to an extinct group which was one of the primitive forms of elephant. The fore limbs of the sirenians, in the form of flippers, have little freedom of movement because of the fusion of the bones of the forearm. The fingers do sometimes carry rudimentary nails, as in the two species, *Trichechus senegalensis* and *Trichechus manatus*.

The teeth are different from the teeth of whales, and most closely resemble those of elephants. There is no external ear. The bones of the nose are either rudimentary or totally absent. For an aquatic animal, the sense of smell is well developed. (whales have no sense of smell). The sirenians can be described as microsmatic (having an under-developed sense of smell) but not anosmatic (having no sense of smell at all). The skull is massive and heavy-boned. All the teeth are molars.

The remainder of the skeleton is massive, like the skull (See Figure 4) and, in general, all the bones are solid. The bones of the spine are all similar in shape. The neck bones are shortened and reduced in number. The usual number is six, although the dugong has seven or eight. The pelvic girdle is shaped like a bow. In some species, there is a rudimentary femur or thigh-bone (See Figure 4).

The tongue is covered with little horny buds, or *papillae*. The stomach is divided. One compartment, known as the cardiac orifice area, is a blind pouch. The second compartment, known as the pyloric area, ends in two blind pouches. The intestine is very long, from 12 to 20 times the body length, and contains an enormous blind pouch. These distinctive features of the teeth and the digestive system are designed for coping with an exclusively vegetarian diet. The *Sirenia* in fact, browse and harvest the beds of seaweed which are abundant on the coasts, estuaries and lower reaches of the rivers.

One species of sirenian has become extinct in recent times; now only two exist. But the two surviving species have each three subspecies or geographical races. The first subspecies of manatee is *Trichechus manatus senegalensis* which is found on the Western rivers of Africa (Figure 5/1). Its tail forms a rounded flipper. It has been suggested that this manatee might well be found in Lake Chad and its river basin, but this hardly seems probable. The second subspecies is *Trichechus manatus manatus*, the Caribbean manatee which ranges from there to the shores of North Brazil and into the Orinoco. The third subspecies is *trichechus manatus inunguis* which has no nails on its flippers and is now found only around the Amazon mouth, although it was once more widespread.

The family *Dugongidae*, also known as *Halicoridae*, includes dugongs and sea cows. The single species of dugong (Figure 5/2) has a fluked tail flipper. It is divided into three subspecies. *Dugong dugong australe*—the Australian *Dugong*

Figure 4: Skeleton of the dugong. See below left the pelvic girdle which is very much reduced in size. A shows that the ribs are not joined underneath to a sternum (floating ribs). After Blainville in P. P. Grassé, Traité de Zoologie.

—is found in Australia and New Guinea. The second, *Dugong dugong dugong*, is found along the coasts of Mozambique to the Philippines. The third is *Dugong dugong hemprichi* from the Red Sea.

The second member of the dugong family was Steller's sea cow which is now extinct. It was the giant of the family, 26 feet in length, and lived in great herds in the Bering Strait and around the Kamchatka Peninsula. It was discovered in 1741 by a Danish navigator in the Russian navy named Vitus Bering, but it was so severely persecuted that it became extinct soon afterwards. In 1963, some Russian fishermen claimed to have seen a Steller's sea cow, but it is now generally accepted that they were mistaken. There is no reason to doubt that the species is extinct.

The appearance of Steller's sea cow (Figure 5/3) can be guessed from fragmentary reconstruction.

The prospects for the sirenians are not bright. With their restricted range and small numbers, they are almost certain to become extinct unless they are given real protection.

Cetacea

These are the mammals best adapted of all for a life in the sea. They are fish-shaped, and spend their entire lives in the water. If they come too near the coast and are stranded, as happens quite frequently with killer whales and sperm whales, they die as the result of their own weight. Their chest cavity flattens and they suffocate.

In the cetaceans, the tail fluke is the propelling organ. It is a horizontal fluke, not vertical, as in fishes. It is composed of strong muscles and connecting tissues. Many of the cetaceans, particularly the dolphins, are so strong that they can leap out of the water and maintain a vertical position, with head and trunk erect. Some of the cetaceans have a triangular dorsal fin, like a shark's, and similar in structure to the tail.

Hind limbs are absent, although they are developed in the embryonic stage. In the fully grown animal, there is little trace of them, no more than the rudiments of certain bones which are not joined to the spinal column. In some species, there is a trace of the thigh bone.

These rudimentary limbs are never visible outside the body.

The arm bones are short, flattened and rigidly joined. The first finger (thumb) is rudimentary. The third and fourth fingers are the most highly developed and elongated by extra joints or phalanges. All the fingers are enclosed in muscular and fatty tissue, forming a pair of fore flippers. These fore flippers are relatively weak and, compared with the powerful tail, are of little help to the animal in swimming.

The skeleton of cetaceans is, overall, rigidly formed along the axis of the skull and back-bone. Most of the bones are rather spongy. As a result, they are comparatively lightweight. The bodies of the animals of this group are heavily encased in blubber and contain a lot of oil and *spermaceti*. *Spermaceti* is a highly valued waxy substance found in the heads of many species. These features all help to explain why such gigantic animals as these are able to float.

Two outstanding features are the absence of external ears and the sealing of the outer ear openings with a wax plug. Ear tubes (eustachian tubes) are, however, present. The eyes are small and have spherical lenses. The nasal passages are also very small and end in a blowhole which is situated on top of the head, not on the snout. In many cetaceans, the part of the brain concerned with the sense of smell is much reduced in size, and without an olfactory nerve. This is true of dolphins which have no sense of smell.

Where teeth are present, they are all of one kind, and range in number, according to species, from 12 to 250. The male of the narwhal has a special canine tooth which it uses to defend itself. Because of this tooth, which can measure from six to eight feet in length, the narwhal has been called the unicorn of the sea. Its other canine tooth does not develop at

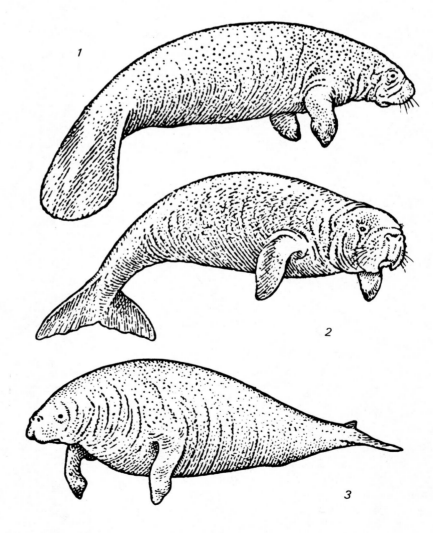

Figure 5: Sirenia *or sea cows:* 1. Trichechus manatus, 2. Dugong dugong, 3. Hydrodamalis Stelleri *(extinct). After* Kosmos-Lexicon *(ed. Herder).*

all. In females, both canines are atrophied.

Cetaceans which have teeth make up the suborder, *Odontoceti*, and are usually ferocious predators on fish and squids. Other cetaceans, like the whales, have only a few teeth which may be reabsorbed before the young animal is born. The newly born young and the adult have no teeth and are classified as the *Mysteceti* (whalebone whales).

These animals feed on plankton, especially certain crustaceans—known as krill—and this is the only food of the biggest whales which are consequently referred to as being *planktotrophic*. As a result of this diet, the palate of these animals has become specially developed. Whales do not chew their food, so their stomachs are divided into three compartments in which it is progressively

digested. The stomach also deals with a vast amount of water.

The skin of cetaceans is smooth and hairless, although traces of hair follicles can be observed in the unborn young. Some species have bristles on the head, known as *vibrissae*, and these are highly sensitive organs of touch. There are no glands on the skin except for those associated with the eyeballs. Female cetaceans have two mammary glands with retracted teats which are noticeable only when the young one is being suckled. During suckling, the nipples are introduced into the young animal's mouth and the milk is ejected by muscular contractions controlled by the mother.

Judged in isolation, the brain of cetaceans is massive, with an average weight of 15 pounds in the blue whale, but its size relative to body size varies greatly from

one species to another. In the *Balaenoptera*, the ratio of brain weight to body weight is 1 to 14,000, while in the *Phocaena*, it is 1 to 105.

Their immense bulk makes it possible for most cetaceans to make prolonged dives to great depths. Their ability to spend long periods under water, without breathing, is due not only to their immense lung capacity, but also to a special myoglobin (responsible for the wine-red shade of the flesh) which provides them with an extra supply of oxygen. The cetaceans, with their red muscles, differ from the *Sirenia* with white muscles in this respect. The white-muscled *Sirenia* have a more limited diving capacity, 10 or 12 minutes at most, despite the fact that they breathe slowly and have a slow heart beat. It is reckoned that they breathe once in 15 to 40 seconds, and that their heart rate is 30 beats per minute.

Whales can be found in great schools or herds that roam the oceans from Polar regions to the Equator. They filter huge volumes of water from which they extract the plankton on which they feed. Dolphins, which are much more intelligent and active than whales, also undertake lengthy migrations in vast schools. They prey upon tuna fish, herring, sardines and squids, which explains the animosity felt towards them by fishermen. Many dolphins tame readily, become affectionate, and are capable of learning. As a result, they have become a great attraction in dolphinariums in recent years.

Nowadays, most species face a real threat of extinction (see Figure 6). The great whales have been the subject of bloody persecution from ancient times. Moby Dick is the classic example of single-minded persecution. The animals are still hunted for their flesh, fats, oils and whalebone. Whalebone is particularly prized in industry because of its strength and flexibility. Even the bones of the animals can be used, so the threat of extinction is a very real one. Only urgent and effective protective measures, at international level, can remove the threat. But whaling is still big business and the future for cetaceans is bleak.

Besides the *Odontoceti* and *Mysteceti*, there is a third suborder of cetaceans, long extinct. This extinct suborder is known as the *Archaeoceti*.

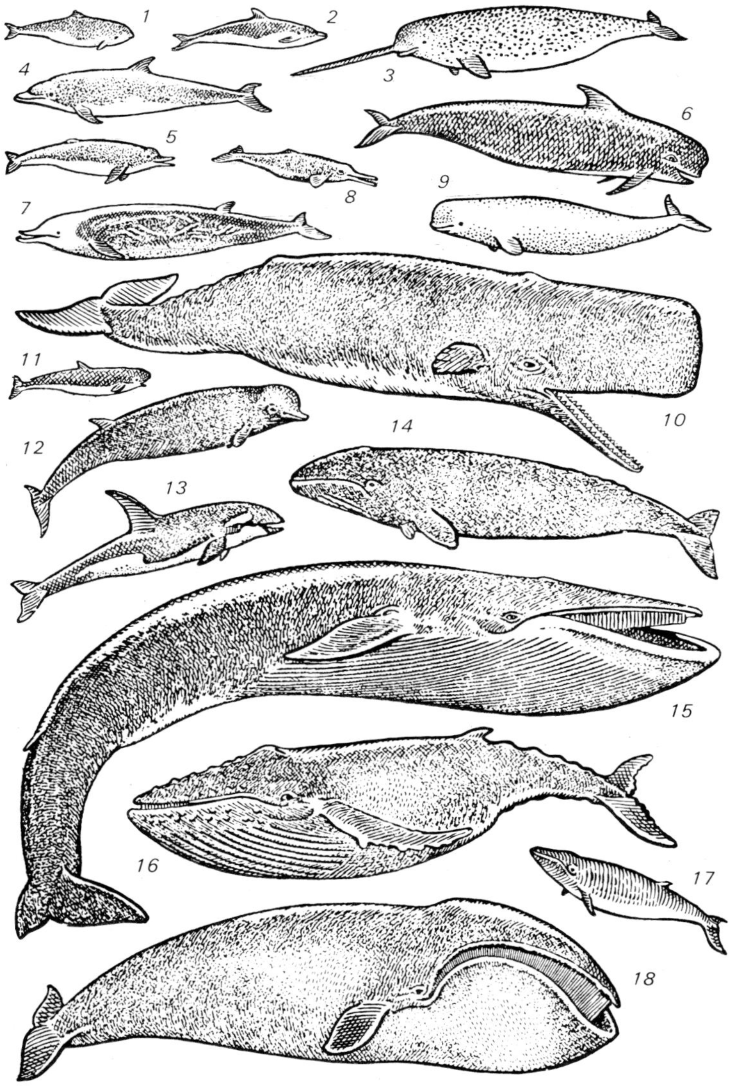

Figure 6: Various species of Cetacea. *Numbers 1 to 9 are shown at* $\frac{1}{100}$ *natural size; numbers 10 to 18 at* $\frac{1}{200}$ *natural size. 1. Phocaena phocaena; 2. Delphinus delphis; 3. Monodon monoceros; 4. Tursiops truncatus; 5. Inia geoffrensis; 6. Globicephala melaena; 7. Ziphius cavirostris; 8. Platanista gangetica; 9. Delphin apterus leucas; 10. Physeter catadon; 11. Kogia breviceps; 12. Hyperoodon ampullatus; 13. Orcinus orca; 14. Eschrichtius glaucus; 15. Balaenoptera musculus; 16. Megaptera novaeangliae; 17. Caperea marginata; 18. Balaena mysticetus.*
After Kosmos-Lexicon *(ed. Herder).*

CONTENTS

Pinnipeds 9
Phocids   12
Gray Seal   16
Elephant Seal   21
Hooded Seal   24
Mediterranean Monk Seal   25
Harp Seal   26
Common Seal   28
Odobenidae   29
Walrus   29
Otariidae   33
Southern Sea Lion   34
California Sea Lion   36
Steller's Sea Lion   44
Alaskan Fur Seal   46
Cape Fur Seal   47

Sirenians   49
Trichechidae   50
Florida Manatee   50
Dugongidae   52
Dugong   52

Cetaceans   56
Mysteceti   62
Balaenidae   62
Greenland Right Whale   62
Balaenopteridae   64
Blue Whale   65
Humpback Whale   66
Common Rorqual   66
Eschrichtidae   68
Odontoceti   68
Phocaenidae   69
Common Porpoise   69
Delphinidae   70
Pilot Whale   70
Killer Whale   71
Dolphin   72
Monodontidae   76
Narwhal   81
Beluga or White Whale   84
Physteridae   86
Sperm Whale or Cachalot   86
Ziphiidae   87
Northern Bottle-Nosed Whale   87
Platanistidae   87
Amazonian Dolphin   88
Gangetic Dolphin or Susu   88

The Pinnipeds

Suborder	Family	*Subfamily*
Pinnipedia	Otaridea	
	Odobenidae	
	Phocidae	*Phocinae* *Lobodontinae* *Monachinae* *Cystophorinae*

In pinnipeds the outer ear is very small or non-existent. The ears, like the nostrils, are simple slits which are closed while the animal is under water.

Pinnipeds

Mammals specially adapted for life in the water. Their bodies are streamlined and their limbs have evolved into flippers.

Class	**Mammalia**
Order	**Carnivora**
Suborder	**Pinnipedia**

Seals, sea lions and walruses are beasts of prey that live and hunt in the sea: marine carnivores. They are known as pinnipeds, which means fin-footed; this is an exact description because they have flippers.

Like the land mammals, they do have legs, arms, hands and feet—inside the flippers. So the flippers are really modified limbs, designed for swimming and diving.

But modification of the limbs is not the only way in which the pinnipeds are adapted to life in the water. Streamlining is another. The body is like a torpedo, perfectly designed for cutting smoothly through water.

Ears and nostrils are specially adapted to an aquatic life involving much diving. During a dive, a special muscle closes the slanting nostrils; another closes the ears, which are either simple holes in the head or have the most rudimentary of ear flaps.

All the pinnipeds are built to withstand long periods in ice-cold water. Under their skins they have a thick layer of fat, often referred to as blubber, which acts as an insulator.

But a thick layer of fat, by itself, would not be enough to enable an animal with a body temperature of 100°F to spend most of its time in the water at 32°F. The pinniped is further helped in reducing heat loss to a minimum by the arrangement of the blood vessels in the flippers and in the fat layer.

In the flippers—which have no insulating fat—as in the fat layer itself, the arteries carrying blood from the heart are in close contact, along their entire length, with the veins bringing blood back to the heart. The wall between arteries and veins is so thin that it conducts heat or cold from one side to the other.

Blood flowing through the arteries to the outermost layers of fat and flippers is progressively cooled by contact with the veins, bringing cold blood from the extremities back to the heart. On its way back the blood in the veins is progressively reheated by contact with the arteries bringing warm blood from the heart.

Another adaptation to life in the sea is the pinnipeds' ability to stay under water for long periods—up to 20 minutes. They cannot breathe under water, as a frog can do. Nor can they take air down with them as the water spider does in its diving bell. This means that they cannot replenish their body oxygen while under water. How, then, can they stay submerged for so long?

They do it by creating an oxygen deficit in certain parts of the body. When the animal dives its heart beat slows down, which puts an automatic brake on the rate of blood circulation. This reduced rate of circulation means that the consumption of oxygen is lowered. In addition to this, the blood supply is shut off from areas of the body where it is not vitally needed.

The only places that receive a normal supply of blood are the heart and brain —the vital organs. The blood is cut off

from the outer arteries supplying the limbs, the skin, and the intestines, and it is in these places that oxygen deficit occurs. The animal does not control these arrangements. It cannot make decisions about them. They are automatic—reflex actions.

The limbs, skin and intestines continue to function despite the abnormal conditions created by lack of oxygen. Once

(Left)
Pinnipeds are carefree animals which spend hours motionless, warming themselves in the sun, well insulated from the ice by their thick layer of fat.

the animal surfaces it replenishes the oxygen in a few breaths. The rate of blood circulation speeds up again. The heart resumes its normal beat. The oxygen deficit is made up, and all parts of the body resume normal function.

After a dive, any pinniped has to surface slowly. This is a purely instinctive safeguard against the condition which is known as "bends" or "divers' sickness" when it occurs in human beings. Pinnipeds are found in all the seas of the world, including the Caspian. They are found even in the great Lake Baikal in Siberia. But they prefer cold water, and the seas richest in number of species and individuals are in the Polar and sub-Polar regions.

Most pinnipeds are found in coastal waters, and some species travel con-

(Above)
The female elephant seal, which is always smaller than the male, does not exceed 11 feet in length and has no trunk.

(Right)
At the end of the last century, the Weddell seal (Leptonychotes Weddelli) was discovered in the Antarctic by the naturalist after whom it is named.

siderable distances up rivers. They are shore-based only at certain times: during the breeding season, and when they haul out to moult or to rest. They young are land-based for the first few weeks of their lives; but their real element is the water, in which they swim and dive with superb grace and ease.

Pinnipeds ashore move clumsily, even with difficulty, dragging themselves laboriously over land and on to rocks. They have the same difficulty when climbing from the water on to ice floes. On land, they move not unlike caterpillars. The animal puts its weight on its chest, heaves its body upwards, rests on its hindquarters, then suddenly stretches out, pushing its shoulders forward almost without using its limbs. The flippers are used for climbing, scratching, grooming, and for cleaning the fur. A nursing female will use her fore flipper like an arm, hugging the young one against her body with it when she dives into the water.

The breeding season is a fasting period that lasts until the females have weaned their young. Hunger then drives the herds seawards and they soon regain their former plump condition.

Most of the pinnipeds are social animals, living in groups at least for the duration of the breeding season. It is most unusual to find one alone. In the most remote areas they remain in very large herds. One species—the Greenland seal—lives in very large colonies, some of them strung out along 30 miles of shore line.

Fur seals and sea lions are found in colonies made up of harems, each of 40 or more females in the charge of one male.

Most seals, however, do not form distinct harems. The harem system is found in species that mate on land, and not even in all of these. In some species there is polygamy but no harem system, the cows associating with individual bulls and exercising free choice in selecting the one with which they will mate. Other species tend towards monogamy. In other words, one bull will associate with only one cow.

In the pinnipeds, as in certain land mammals, there is the phenomenon of delayed implantation. This means that the fertilized egg, in the first instance, develops in the uterus (womb) for only a short period. Development stops when the "fertile" egg reaches the stage known as a *blastocyst*. No further development of the young can take place until this *blastocyst* becomes implanted, or bedded, in the uterine wall. In the pinnipeds implantation does not take place immediately. There is a period of delay, which varies from species to species. Hence the term "delayed implantation." Once implantation has taken place, development proceeds normally. The period of gestation is from eight to twelve months, according to species.

Female pinnipeds usually give birth to a single pup; but twins occur on rare occasions.

Pinnipeds are almost entirely marine, and species living in fresh water are rare. The suborder (or order, as some scientists would have it) is divided into three families—*phocids, odobenids* and *otariids*—comprising about 30 species.

Phocids

Seals with no external ear. Their hind flippers point permanently backwards.

Class	**Mammalia**
Order	**Carnivora**
Suborder	**Pinnipedia**
Family	**Phocidae**

The seals in this group have no external ear. The first or marginal digit (finger) is longer than the

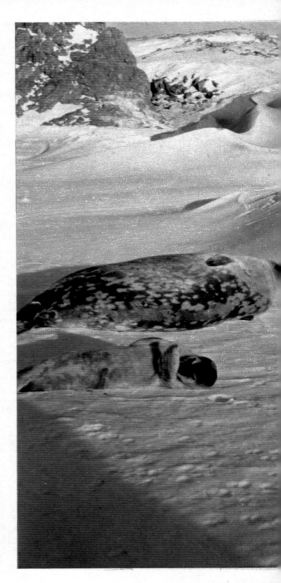

(Above and right)
Pinnipeds usually have only one pup, very rarely two. Most are born covered in soft thick fur which they lose after a few weeks.

(Right-hand page, top)
In winter, when the sea is completely frozen over, the seals make holes in the ice through which they can enter and leave the water. They have to surface to breathe.

(Right)
Pinnipeds are born well developed after a very long gestation period. The mother's milk is particularly rich and the suckling period is short.

others. **There are claws on all digits, front and rear. The hind limbs always point backwards, and have little freedom of movement, so are of no help to the animal when it is ashore.** The coat is made up of stiff hairs, and, in some cases, there is a sparse under-fur. In most species the coat is spotted.

Many of the seals in this group are named after land mammals to which they bear some kind of resemblance. For example, the leopard seal is so called because of its markings. The elephant seal is so called because of its trunk-like nose, reminding one of the trunk of an elephant.

Phocids are the most widely distributed of pinnipeds. They are found in all the world's seas, and a few are found in inland waters that are still linked with the sea by rivers, or which were at one time part of the sea. The Caspian Sea and Lake Baikal are two such places.

In the water, the phocids move with the greatest of ease. They are fast swimmers, and can remain floating for hours, motionless or even asleep, with only their heads and part of their backs showing above the surface. On land, they drag themselves along slowly and laboriously.

They can dive to a great depth. If they are hunting or playing, and are in no danger, they will surface to breathe at intervals of 15 to 25 seconds. If they are under threat, or being hunted, they will stay under water for several minutes at a time. When ashore, and resting, they breathe at intervals of five to eight seconds. When a herd is asleep on shore, there are always a few animals awake, on guard.

Although seals can stay in the sea for days, and even weeks at a time, they still like to haul out to rest or sleep or bask in the sun. When basking, they lie on their sides, or on their bellies, or even on their backs, when they look like giant slugs. Fierce battles often take place between bulls fighting for the best places ashore. Although their movements on land are laborious and awkward, seals can move with considerable speed over a short distance. It takes an agile man to catch up with one when

it is making its escape to the water.

In Arctic regions, the seals more often lie on ice floes than on rocks. When hauled out on ice, they will lie motionless for hours at a time, just as they do on the rocks. Their thick layer of fat allows them to lie on ice without discomfort. But all of them like to lie and bask in the warmth of the sun.

During the severest part of the winter, when great areas of the sea are frozen over, the seals make breathing holes in the ice. They make these holes as soon as the ice begins to form and keep them open afterwards. They use the holes for getting into the water to hunt, and as an exit back to the ice. This constant two-way traffic ensures that the holes do not freeze over.

Phocids have a considerable vocal range. Their normal call is a raucous bark, but they have another call resembling the mooing of a cow. An angry seal can growl like a dog and, when really roused, it will roar noisily.

The senses are generally well developed, sight being the most acute, with hearing taking second place. Sense of smell is

14

The phocids' true element is water, in which they move with amazing ease. They can spend several weeks without hauling out on land.

not so well developed and would, in any case, be of no use to the animal under water; it is sufficiently well developed, however, for the seal to detect approaching danger on land by smell alone. Touch is sufficiently developed for the animal to detect a foreign body in the water on the slightest contact. The long strong hairs on the lower lip, known as *vibrissae*, are highly sensitive.

The nose and ears can be closed at will by muscular movement. The nostrils open each time the animal breathes, and close again immediately. The ear holes are automatically sealed under water.

The irises, which are large and slightly convex, occupy almost all of the space between the eyelids, so that it is most unusual to see the white of a seal's eye.

Seals can be easily tamed. They quickly learn to respond to their name and will come when called, taking food from the hand. In the wild state, they appear to be usually non-aggressive towards other species apart, of course, from those on which they prey—fish, molluscs and crabs. In captivity, they show a marked hostility towards dogs.

The seal cow is a good mother. She plays a great deal with her pup and is always ready to defend it courageously against enemies. When danger threatens, the cow will take her pup in her fore flippers and hold it closely to her, swimming seawards with it. A cow will flipper a pup out of dangerous water to safety.

(Top)
*The leopard seal (*Hydrurga leptonyx*) is a particularly aggressive species that lives in southern waters. It eats penguins and young seals of other species.*

(Right)
In phocids the external ear has completely disappeared; this cuts down heat loss and improves the body's streamlining.

Gray Seal

The gray seal, also known as the Atlantic seal, is a North Atlantic species. There are breeding colonies on the coasts of Nova Scotia, Labrador, Norway, Finland and in the British Isles.

The world population of gray seals is under 40,000, and three out of four are found in British waters. The largest breeding colonies are on the Scottish islands of North Rona and Orkney, and the Farne Islands off the north-east coast of England.

There is a lot of variation in the coats and in the markings of this species. Bull seals vary from near black or dark brown or gray, with lighter spots or patches; females are light gray or brown with darker spots. Bulls are larger and much heavier than cows, measuring between seven and eight feet in length, and weighing between 650 and 900 pounds. Cows measure from six feet to just over seven feet in length, and weigh between 375 and 550 pounds. The pup of the seal is stained yellowish or ochreous at birth, but the fur whitens quickly on clean ground. The white coat is moulted from the age of three weeks and is replaced by the dark sea-going coat by the age of five weeks. Bull seals moult from March to May;

In the Arctic, the breeding season is in late autumn. Farther south, it takes place in April, May and June. Pregnancy in seals lasts from eight to ten months, and a single pup is usual, although occasionally a female will have twins. Seal pups are born on islands, sandy beaches, ice floes and mud flats. The white fur of the newly born pup is soon replaced by the juvenile fur which is its sea-going coat. The mother remains ashore with her pup until it has moulted into this sea-going coat.

In a few weeks, the young seals resemble the adults in every way except size. In northern regions, the pups keep their birth coat longer than those in the south. In early life, the young seals eat mainly crabs and other small marine animals, especially molluscs. Later they begin to catch fish—about 11 pounds a day. They will also take water fowl.

The phocid seals in the far north are much hunted. They are killed for their fur, fat and meat. Seal hunting is still big business, especially during the period when the animals are at their breeding stations.

All the phocids can survive severe wounding and mutilation. Apart from man, their most formidable enemy is the killer whale. They are also hunted by polar bears, and young seals are sometimes killed by large predatory fish.

There are some 20 species of phocids, widespread in the northern hemisphere. Of these, we shall look at six—the gray seal, the elephant seal, the hooded seal, the monk seal, the harp seal and the common seal.

(Top)
The Weddell seal is less gregarious than other seals. It is found in the Antarctic—on the Kerguelen Islands at the extreme south of New Zealand and of South America.

(Above)
Elephant seals mate on land, shortly after the cows have given birth to their pups. Pregnancy lasts nearly a year.

(Right)
Gray seal pup, moulter, in its first sea-going coat.

cow seals from January to March.

Gray seals are marine and offshore animals that come ashore to breed. They like islands and rocky shores, and usually stay close to the water's edge. Despite being awkward on land, the animals in some colonies will scramble up steep slopes and cliffs to breeding stations 300 feet above sea level.

The pups are born in early autumn or early winter, the actual time of birth varying from colony to colony. Weight at birth varies from 20 to 40 pounds. There are no records of twins. Because of the richness of seal milk, which is almost two-thirds solids, the pups grow at the rate of four pounds a day, and reach 70 to 100 pounds at the end of two weeks. The milk teeth are shed before birth; the adult teeth appear a day or two later. Pups are weaned at the age of three weeks, when they begin their first moult.

In this species, there is no strict harem system. The bull defends his territory, while the cow holds the area around her pup. She has considerable freedom of movement and can mate with any bull she chooses. At the beginning of the season, a bull may have as many as 50 cows on his territory; later he may have less than half that number.

The cows mate after weaning their pups and return to the sea where they begin to feed after their three week's fast. The bulls may fast for the whole two months of the breeding season.

There are many casualties among gray seal pups in the early days. A very young pup falling into the sea is in real difficulty if the cow is not at hand to rescue it, and it may drown after many vain efforts to scramble ashore. Gray seal pups cannot tread water until they are four or five weeks old. But the gray seal is a devoted mother, and will rescue her young, using her flippers like arms, and her body as a shield against the waves. One cow was observed escorting her week-old pup in heavy seas round the island of North Rona and bringing it ashore in calm water to leeward—a sea journey of two miles.

Considered on a world basis the gray seal is a rare animal. In Great Britain, which has three-quarters of the world population, the species is protected.

Elephant Seal

The southern elephant seal is the largest phocid—females reaching a length of 12 feet and males 21 feet. Males can reach a weight of over three tons.

The head of this seal is large and long. The broad muzzle extends to form a kind of trunk—hence its name—and its upper lip has brown whiskers about six inches in length. The eyes are large and prominent, with eyebrows of stiff hair.

The ear, situated behind and below the eye, is no more than a hole in the head, with no ear flap. The nose varies in length according to sex and age. In mature bulls, it is a trunk about 16 inches long and this can double its size when the animal is aroused. At rest, the trunk hangs down limply with the nostril opening towards the ground.

The body is thick-set and muscular, with no obvious neck, and the spine is so flexible that the seal can reach its rump with its muzzle. The fore flippers are strong and sturdy, with the fingers joined together to form a fin. The powerful hind flippers are five-fingered and deeply notched in the middle. They are used as oars. There are strong, blunt claws on the fore flippers. The tail is short and pointed. The coat, which consists of short stiff hairs, varies from gray-blue to white according to age, sex and time of year.

Elephant seals range over the South Atlantic and Pacific, spending the summer on small islands where they can breed and moult.

In late autumn and winter, they go back to the sea. At this stage, they are thought to be migratory; but the extent and the course of their migration are not known.

Along the coasts of California, Mexico and Guadeloupe, the ranges of the northern and southern elephant seals overlap.

Elephant seals like to haul out on sandy beaches or pebbly beaches. But they move with great difficulty on shore and tire quickly. Like all seals, the elephant seal progresses by caterpillar movements, arching and straightening its body alternately and leaving deep furrows in the sand. In water it moves with ease and grace, and at high speed when hunting prey—fish and cuttle-fishes. Sometimes it feeds on algae. It can sleep tranquilly on the roughest sea.

Elephant seals are calm, peaceful creatures, not given to hostility without violent provocation. Their intelligence cannot compare with that of other seals and sea lions.

The period of gestation in this species is

(Pages 18–19)
Phocids' hind flippers always point backwards; they are useless to the animals on land.

(Left)
At birth young phocids are clad in a thick coat of fine white fur which is highly prized by the fur trade. After a few weeks this coat is replaced by rougher fur which is often spotted.

(Above)
After a few months on land, by which time the young elephant seals are able to fend for themselves, the whole colony takes to the sea again.

about 340 days, and mating takes place soon after the birth of the young. There is, of course, delayed implantation. The very short interval between the birth of the pup and the mating of the mother is made possible, as in other phocids, because the uterus (womb) has two horns that function alternately. One is always ready to function in the act of mating while the other is recovering from that of giving birth.

Female elephant seals reach their breeding stations between the end of August and the beginning of October. Soon after arrival they form groups of about 20. A week or so later the cows give birth to their single pup. The pup at birth weighs from 90 to 110 pounds and measures about four feet in length. Its coat at birth is black and fluffy. Within two weeks or so, it moults this for a light gray one. The suckling period is about five weeks, during which the pup makes rapid growth. At the age of three or four months, the young seal can swim perfectly and is completely at home in the water. The males reach the age of three years before the trunk begins to show.

The life span is about 30 years. Bull elephant seals do not form their harems until the pups are arriving. Pupping takes place for a period of about a month and the bulls begin to challenge and fight soon after the first one is born. In most cases, battles between bulls are rituals. They are displays more than battles, and both animals play the game according to the rules. Conflict ends as soon as one bull submits and breaks off. There is no pursuit.

Battles between males are accompanied by much roaring but little actual fighting. However, if the adversaries are equally strong, the fight can become more serious. Then they try to bite each other on the trunk and neck. Defeated bulls are not allowed to hold a harem and are relegated to join the outcasts of the colony. But they are not permanently excluded. They remain on the alert, always ready to take over from a harem bull, or *pasha*, the moment he falters or loses interest. Elephant seals mate on land.

The harem territories are as closely situated as houses in a street. During this period, the bulls do not feed, but spend all their time guarding the frontiers of their territory, mating with, and supervising, their cows. This system does not apply to virgin cows, which arrive at the breeding station later than the pregnant ones. When all the harems

(Top)
Elephant seals spend only a few months on land—the time needed to give birth to their young, to rear them and to mate. They return to land in February in order to moult.

(Left)
The northern elephant seal (Mirounga augustirostris) is found on the coasts of California, Mexico and Guadeloupe.

(Right-hand page, top)
The male elephant seal's nose forms a trunk some 15 inches long which doubles its length when the animal is aroused.

have been set up, these virgin cows are mated by non-harem, non-territorial bulls. At the end of November, the harem system breaks up and all the seals return to the sea.

About the end of January, the seals return to the beaches to moult; but this time the groups separate by sex—the bull seals on one part of the island and the cows on another. Their skins begin to peel and they roll on the ground to hasten the stripping process. As soon as the new fur has grown in, the seals go back to the sea and remain there until the following breeding season.

The world population of elephant seals is between 400,000 and 600,000. Man still hunts this species wherever he finds it. The thick hard skin, with its covering of short hair, is suitable for the manufacture of suitcases, harnesses and other articles. And so the killing goes on.

Hooded Seal

The hooded seal is found in the Arctic Ocean and the North Atlantic, especially along the coasts of North America, Greenland and the surrounding islands. On the coast of Greenland, it is more often found on the vast ice floes than on land.

(Right)
During the mating season elephant seals become fighters. The bulls meet in single combat before an audience of indifferent females.

The bull of this species can be distinguished from all other pinnipeds by the hood from which he derives his name. This hood is found only in males over the age of four years. It is a leathery pouch, extending from nose to crown, which can be inflated by the animal at will.

This adornment gives the species its other name of bladder-nose. The bladder originates in the nasal cavity. The bull seal inflates two red pockets which balloon out from the nostrils to form a hood up to ten inches long and eight inches high. It reaches its maximum size when he is excited or displaying.

The bull hooded seal reaches a length of eight feet but females do not exceed six and a half feet. The head is large and the muzzle rounded. In other respects, hooded seals are like other pinnipeds. The claws are sturdy; the tail is short and wide. The outer coat is composed of long hairs, overlying a dense woolly under-fur. It is brownish on the back, gray or rust on the underside.

From September to March, hooded seals are found in the Davis Strait and Baffin Bay where they feed on the numerous fish and cephalopods. In April or May, they appear off the Greenland coast, and remain there until the end of June or the beginning of July. During this time the seals moult, the young are born and the cows mate again. After the breeding season, the seals undertake their annual northward migration.

Pregnancy in this species lasts about a year. Before birth, the seal pup moults its first coat, which comes away with the

(Top)
Like most phocids, elephant seals show great affection for their young. They look after them and play with them a great deal.

(Above)
Elephant seals have a single pup, which is black at birth. It loses this first fur at the age of two weeks when it becomes gray. It is suckled by its mother for five weeks.

afterbirth. The name "afterbirth" is given to the placenta and membranes attaching the unborn animal to its mother inside the womb. The pup's birth fur is white, and it keeps this coat until it is a year old. The white fur is valuable in the fur trade, and animals under a year old are much sought after by hunters.

Like other male seals, bull hooded seals engage in furious battles, bellowing and inflating their hoods.

The present world population of hooded seals is estimated at 400,000. About 3,000 animals are killed annually.

Mediterranean Monk Seal (*Monachus monachus*)

Most seals live in the cold northern seas, where there is abundance of plankton, and therefore an abundance of the fish and cephalopods on which they feed.

The Mediterranean monk seal, on the other hand, is found in the Mediterranean, the Black Sea and the Adriatic; along the west coast of Africa as far as the Rio de Oro; and around the Canary Islands.

Another species (*Monachus schauinslandi*) is found in the Pacific, in the region of the Hawaiian Islands. A third species (*Monachus tropicalis*) which may now be extinct, was found in the Gulf of Mexico and the Caribbean.

Bull monk seals measure up to ten feet in length; females are slightly smaller. Weight ranges, in adults, from 500 to 600 pounds. The adult fur, composed of rough short hair with no under-fur, is more or less uniformly grayish brown, paling to yellow or grayish white on the under parts. Pups are lighter in hue.

Monk seals like to haul out on rocky islets along precipitous coasts, and are especially attracted to cliffs with sea caves that flood at high tide. Their food consists mainly of fish, molluscs and crustaceans. Nowadays, they are mostly found in small family groups, or even pairs. If not disturbed, they remain happily in the one place. They are timid

animals whose habits are little known, partly because they are so difficult to observe and partly because of their great rarity.

Cow monk seals give birth to a single pup in August or September, after a pregnancy of 11 months. The pup's birth coat is black. The cow chooses an inaccessible place, or a sea cave, to give birth to her pup, which she nurses for three or four weeks. At the age of six weeks, the pup is independent.

The monk seal's cry is a prolonged bark repeated several times. It can also howl noisily and utter a sound like a human sneeze.

Threatened with extinction, this species is now protected by law. The present population in the Mediterranean is estimated at about 500.

(Top)
The monk seal has become so rare that it now lives alone or in small family groups. Threatened with extinction, it is protected by law. There are perhaps fewer than 500 left in the Mediterranean.

(Above)
The Mediterranean monk seal lives mostly in the Mediterranean and the Black Sea ringed in green, the West Indian monk seal in the Caribbean, ringed in red, and the Hawaiian in the Hawaiian Islands, ringed in blue.

Harp Seal

The harp seal or saddleback *(Phoca groenlandica)* **measures up to six feet in length and weighs about 400 pounds.**

The outer fur is dense, short and smooth, covering a woolly under-fur. In adult males the coat is grayish fawn or sometimes a faint, light yellow.

The front of the head and the muzzle are blackish brown or chocolate.

On his back, the bull carries the harp, sometimes more like a long horse-shoe, from which he derives his name. The harp marking is dark like the muzzle, and therefore distinctive. In the smaller, paler female, its pattern is less obvious.

The harp seal is a true northern seal whose habitat is limited to the icy waters of the Arctic and the North Atlantic Oceans. It avoids dry land at all times, living entirely on and under the ice floes that stretch to the horizon. It keeps open breathing holes in the ice, and uses them for entering and leaving the water. These breathing holes are visited regularly by its two predators—the polar bear and the human seal hunter.

There are three great herds of harp seals in the world, each occupying a clearly demarcated area of the sea. One herd spends the winter around the coast of Newfoundland; another frequents the coast of Iceland; the third is found in the

White Sea. In spring, when the ice begins to melt, the herds migrate Northwards. Even then, they do not seem to mix or make contact.

The period of gestation is 11 months. Pups are born in the spring, on ice thick enough to carry the weight of the cow and her young. Soon after the birth of their pups, the cows mate with the bulls. After mating, the bulls return to the sea. Cows usually give birth to a single pup, but some hunters claim to have seen twins and triplets. Such claims probably arise from the fact that the harp seal cow will readily suckle an orphaned pup.

The pups are born in an advanced stage of development, and have a dense white fleece. For the first few days of their lives, they lie stretched out on the ice, sleeping and being suckled. At this stage,

they cannot swim. Their white fur helps to camouflage them.

They make rapid growth and soon moult their white fur for a spotted coat. When they have completed their moult, they take to the water where their mothers teach them to swim and fish. They moult again during the summer, after which they resemble the adults.

Unlike other seals, the harp seal can use its fore flippers as real feet. In water, it is extraordinarily fast and often makes haste by leaping into the air. This habit of the harp seals may explain the frequent sightings of supposed gigantic sea serpents. In the open sea, these seals sometimes swim in Indian file and, if they all leap into the air at the same time, in synchronized movement, they could well give the impression of a long serpent caterpillaring over the waves.

(Left)
Harp seals live in the icy waters of the Arctic Ocean. There they form huge herds which never leave the coldest waters.

(Top)
Harp seals live under the ice. They maintain holes in the ice through which they can surface to breathe.

(Above)
Harp seal pups are born well developed and clad in a dense white fleece.

Common Seal

The common seal *(Phoca vitulina)* **is not a seal of the ice floes, being found in more temperate areas of the Arctic, and on the coasts of Northern Europe, Asia and America.**

It is found everywhere off the British coast, and has been reported from France. Seal Lake, in Canada, which is 2,600 feet above sea level, has supported a flourishing colony since time immemorial, and there is no evidence that the seals have suffered any ill effects through being cut off from the sea. There is also a colony on a fresh-water lake in Alaska, but there is a water link with the Bering Sea, which the seals can reach any time they want to.

This is a less gregarious species than most of the others, and is never found in great colonies concentrated on a single beach. Common seals are also greater stay-at-

homes, moving within a radius of five to ten miles from their home beach. The main food is flat fish, molluscs and crustaceans.

Female common seals reach puberty at the age of two years, males at four years. The gestation period is shorter than in other seals and is reckoned to be about 280 days. Mating takes place in the water and the date varies according to geography. Implantation takes place in November and December, and pups are born in June and July.

The pup moults its first coat before birth. A few, however, retain the white coat for a few days after birth while others are born with only a few white hairs.

Common seals reach a length of six feet and a weight of 260 pounds. Pups weigh between 20 and 30 pounds at birth, and measure from 31 to 35 inches.

Apart from man, the common seal's main enemies are the polar bear and the killer whale.

(Top)
Common seals are sociable but less gregarious than other seals. They are never found in huge colonies huddled together on the same beach.

(Left)
Common seals live in fresh water as well as in sea water. In captivity they settle down well and become very tame.

Odobenids

<table>
<tr><td>The walrus is the only living species in this family. Walruses have less streamlined bodies than other pinnipeds, and a swollen midriff.</td></tr>
</table>

Class	Mammalia
Order	Carnivora
Suborder	Pinnipedia
Family	Odobenidae

In this family, there is only a single living species—the walrus.

The walrus has no external ears. The fore flippers have no claws. Unlike the seals, the walrus can move its hind limbs forward, so they can be used while the animal is moving about on land. The teeth are under-developed, with the exception of the upper canines which grow into tusks.

The tusks appear, in both sexes, at the age of four months. The teeth are arranged, upper and lower, on each side of the jaw, as follows:

incisors $\frac{3}{3}$ canines $\frac{1}{1}$

pre-molars $\frac{4}{4}$ molars $\frac{1}{0}$

Walrus

The walrus (Odobenus rosmarus) **can reach a length of 13 feet and can weigh over a ton. The female is a third smaller than the male.**

The head is relatively small and round. The muzzle is short and wide, and has 400 evenly distributed whiskers which are as strong as the quills of a hen and nearly 12 inches long. The whiskers are highly sensitive and are used as organs of touch—perhaps also as filters when the animal is fishing on muddy bottoms.

The walrus is notable for its great upper canine teeth which grow into down-pointing tusks. At a year old, the walrus's tusks are about an inch long; at two years, they are five inches long; at five years old, they are 14 inches long. In adult males, they may reach a length of three feet, and weigh up to 13 pounds.

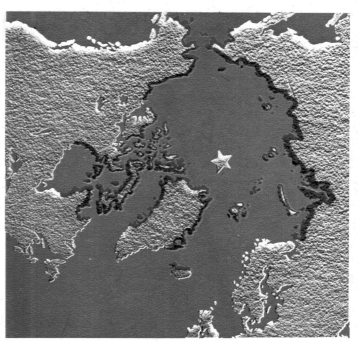

(Top)
The walrus is polygamous, but does not form harems. It is the only pinniped that breeds only once every two years.

(Above)
Today the walrus is confined to Greenland and the Bering Strait. It was formerly found as far south as Scotland.

29

The maximum tusk length in females is two feet.

Contrary to popular belief, the walrus's tusks are not used for walking on land, despite the fact that the Greek name means, literally, "walking teeth". Nor are they used—except perhaps by old bulls—to defend themselves or to attack. They are used mainly for foraging on the sea bed, although a cow will use her tusks for gathering her young against her body.

The main diet of walruses consists of molluscs and crustaceans, and the animals use their tusks for tearing these creatures from rocks and from the sea bottom.

They kill bigger prey by holding it between their front flippers and crushing it. Some Arctic explorers have testified that the walrus can tear open the belly of a polar bear with its tusks.

The walrus's rough flaccid skin seems too big for its body, almost like a boy in a man's coat. The skin's thickness increases with age and, in old bulls, may exceed two and a half inches. There is a sparse covering of red hair, but very old animals are almost bald. Under the skin, there is a layer of fat which may reach a thickness of four inches and weigh 990 pounds.

Walruses are found in the Arctic Ocean in ice-free waters, but close to the ice edge, which they hardly ever leave. They were at one time, however, found on the coast of Scotland, and exceptionally in the Thames estuary. They keep to the coasts, avoiding the open sea as far as possible.

The home range of the walrus is the Arctic—the coast of Siberia, from the mouth of the Yenisey River to the islands of Novaya Zemlya and Spitsbergen, Greenland and the coast of Hudson Bay. Nevertheless, some animals wander far from their home, and walruses have been killed in Denmark, the Netherlands, Norway and Scotland.

When swimming, the walrus uses its fore flippers for propulsion, and can reach a speed of 15 miles per hour—that is 13 knots.

Walruses live a gregarious, peaceful and carefree life, pasturing on the crustaceans and molluscs of the sea bed, like cattle in a meadow. They group by sex, males crowding together in one place, the

(Top)
Walruses live in the parts of the Arctic Ocean which are free of ice and now hardly venture beyond the ice edge.

(Left and right)
Male and female walruses have tusks which can reach a length of three feet and a weight of nearly 13 pounds. The tusks are canine teeth.

females with their pups in another. The groups herd so closely that the overcrowding sometimes results in broken bones. When the animals are sleeping, there is always one on guard to warn of the approach of danger. Only walruses that have already had experience of man are disturbed by the approach of a ship.

The intelligence of the walrus is not rated highly. Its sight is poor, its hearing only a little better. The sense of smell is the most highly developed, enabling it to scent danger several hundred feet away.

During the mating season, which is in June and July, the bulls engage in fierce battles and many of them are scarred for life. They are probably polygamous, but do not form organized harems. Some bulls appear to have only one cow, and there are many families of a bull, cow and young.

The nursing period is long, lasting two years or more. The female walrus is the only pinniped that does not breed every year; she has a pup every second year. On rare occasions, a female may have twins. Pregnancy lasts between 11 and 12 months.

Pups are born in the sea, and the pupping period extends from April to June. At birth, the pup is three and a half feet long and weighs about 110 pounds. It has a coat of thick gray down. At this stage, it clings to its mother's neck and is cared for with great tenderness. The mother is always ready to defend her pup.

Females reach puberty at the age of four or five years; males at the age of five or six years. The life span is not known with certainty; but has been estimated at from 16 to 30 years.

Up to the end of the nineteenth century, the Eskimoes hunted the walrus, using its fat for food and fuel. Its meat, though oily and leathery, was considered a great delicacy. The skin was used for making straps and tents for summer camps. The bones were used to make tools, and the tusks for ivory.

There has been a drastic decline in the walrus population over the last century, and the world total is now reckoned at between 50,000 and 100,000. The decline still goes on, but attempts are now being made to reach international agreement to halt it.

(Above, left)
Young walruses do not have tusks, but they already have flourishing moustaches.

32

Otariidae

**Otariidae make up the third and last
family of the suborder of pinnipeds.
All the animals in this family have
a small but well developed external
ear—an ear-flap that is recognizable
as such. They also have a long clearly
defined neck, enabling the animal to
turn its head in any direction.**
The hind limbs can be brought forward
to act as hind feet. The flippers are sturdy.
The feet, which are long and oar-shaped,
have naked soles with a furrow along
their length. The toes of the hind flippers
are all about the same length, while the
clawless toes of the fore flippers become
progressively shorter from the inside
out.

The hind flippers are used as rudders,
while the fore flippers oar the animal
through the water. On dry land, all four
limbs are used for locomotion, assisted
by a swaying motion of the long neck.
Under the skin, the otariids have
sebaceous glands—the sweat glands of
the land mammals—whose secretions
cover the skin with a waterproof film.
Inside the ears, there are solidified
secretions that probably perform a
similar task.

Some of the otaries have sparse shaggy
fur which, in males, forms a neck mane.
This neck mane is the origin of the name
sea lion (the sub-family *Otariinae*). Other
otariids have a denser, more glossy coat,
and are known as fur seals (the sub-
family *Arctocephalinae*).
In the fur seals, the fur is different from
that of other seals. The hair grows in
tufts. Each long supple hair is surrounded
by shorter ones. These hairs grow from
different follicles, but from the same
pore, and there is no muscle enabling
them to be erected. At each moult, the

fur seal will lose only half of his hairs.
Otariids have the strange habit of
swallowing stones, many of which are
certainly swallowed accidentally. But
others are obviously swallowed voluntarily, because stones have been found
in the stomachs of pups that are still
being suckled.

Many theories have been advanced to
explain this habit. It has been suggested
that the stones may soothe the irritation
caused by intestinal worms; they may
even help to grind up the food. Many
fishermen believe that they act as ballast,
helping the otariids to dive. The most
recent, and apparently the most plausible,
theory is that the stones lessen the discomfort of the contractions of an empty
stomach in animals that sometimes spend
long periods without eating.
We shall now look at three members of
the Otariinae—the southern sea lion,
the California sea lion and the northern
sea lion. Then we shall look at two
members of the *Arctocephalinae*—the
Alaskan fur seal and the Cape fur seal.

(Left)
*Walrus pups weigh 110 pounds at birth and
are not mature until they are five years old.
They are born in the sea and are suckled by
their mothers for more than two years.*

(Above)
*Female otaries are incorporated into the
harems when they come ashore. They give
birth to the pups conceived the preceding
year. The harem bull defends the pups,
although they were probably fathered by
another bull.*

33

Southern Sea Lion

The southern sea lion *(Otariinae byronia)* **has short ears and a rough coat which, in adult males, forms a mane reaching down to the shoulders.**

The fur is generally brown, the flippers being darker than the body; but there is great variation according to age and sex, and between individuals of the same age and sex. In fact, the coat ranges from dark brown to yellow and gold and cream. This variation has led to much confusion and to many arguments as to the number of sub-species.

The young of both sexes have a thin woolly chocolate-brown coat. Adult males reach a length of eight feet and weigh up to 110 pounds; females measure up to six feet in length and are correspondingly lighter in weight.

This sea lion is found in the southern hemisphere—Antarctica, Tierra del Fuego and Patagonia. It occurs as far south as Graham Land, and as far north as Peru and Brazil. Although a marine animal, it sometimes travels up rivers, and has been recorded 180 miles upstream from the mouth of the River Plate.

Each year, the southern sea lion undertakes the long migration to its breeding grounds, on the South American mainland and the Falkland Islands. On the Argentine coast, there are about 60 breeding stations, with a total population of 200,000. The Falkland population is about 400,000. There are 200,000 on other parts of the South American mainland, so the world population is over 800,000, and may be over a million.

The breeding rookeries of the southern sea lion are fixed: in other words the animals return to the same places year after year. At the rookeries, they crowd in serried ranks, each bull stamping out a small territory which he defends fiercely against other males. After the establishment of these territories, the cows arrive with their one-year-old pups, and this gives rise to renewed fighting among the males. Each male holds a harem of seven or eight cows. Non-harem bulls, too young or not strong enough to hold territory, form separate groups.

Throughout the breeding season, the bulls defend their territories and harems. Although there is no physical boundary between the territories, the harem bulls defend the area as though it were clearly demarcated. Any bull attempting to steal cows from another bull's harem is driven off by aggressive display or attack.

The harem bulls are never at rest. They patrol their boundaries, appear to lose interest in food, and hardly ever close their eyes. So the rookery is noisy right round the clock. After two or three months, the harem bulls are in a state of almost complete exhaustion. Their body fat disappears so that their skin slackens and hangs on them in great folds. It takes two months of abundant sea feeding to restore their weight and vitality.

The main food of these sea lions is small fish and squids. They have few enemies apart from the leopard seal *(Hydrurga leptonyx)* which is sometimes a predator on pups. But the main deaths among sea lion pups are caused by the huge bulls of their own species rolling on them and crushing them while they lie asleep.

Sea lions are noisy and vocal, uttering a variety of calls. Early in the mating season, the bulls roar. When fighting, they growl at each other and bark. They can also spit like angry cats.

Before the act of mating, the southern sea lion performs a courtship ritual in which sensuous body movements play

(Top)
The arrival of the southern sea lion females at the rookeries gives rise to fierce fights between males setting up their harems.

(Left)
The southern sea lion is clad in a fairly thin rough coat which is usually brown.

an important role. Cows come into breeding condition soon after the birth of their pups, and they are mated within a week. Once he has mated all his cows, the pasha bull relaxes his vigilance and the harem system gradually breaks down.

Pregnancy lasts a year. Pups are born between December 25th and January 15th. At birth, they are three feet long and completely black. They are suckled for six months, during which time their mother defends them courageously against all dangers.

The first three months of the pups' lives are spent in exploring their surroundings and in mock hunting. At the age of four months, they begin to play with nearby objects. Males grow their mane at the age of four years, but they are not mature until the age of six. Females are mature at the age of four years. The life span is between 17 and 20 years.

Because of the remoteness of their breeding stations. There has been no systematic massacres as in other pinnipeds. Nevertheless, since the sixteenth century, they have been killed in Argentina and Paraguay for their fat, skin and meat.

(Above)
Southern sea lion males have a mane.
Females have none.

California Sea Lion

The California sea lion (*Zalophus Californiaus*) **is a graceful streamlined animal, half the size of the southern species.**

This is the familiar sea lion, the one so often referred to as the performing seal.

The largest males of this species measure up to six and a half feet in length and weigh about 400 pounds. Females are smaller and slimmer, and weigh about 200 pounds. This species has a receding forehead. The California sea lion has a bony crest on the top of its skull.

California sea lions are found in great numbers round the coast of California, and especially in the Gulf of California and on nearby islands. A sub-species (*Zalophus Californiaus Japonicus*) is found in Japanese waters—in the southern part of the sea of Japan around Honshu Island, Sakishima and Saki.

Yet another sub-species (*Zalophus Californiaus mollebrachi*) is found in the Galapagos Islands.

The California sea lion differs little from the southern sea lion in general habits. The harems are made up in the same way. The bull patrols his territory as constantly. Mating takes place within a few days of the birth of the pups. Unlike many carnivores, the female does not eat the afterbirth.

In California, the sea lion pups are born in May and June. On the Galapagos, they are born between October and December. Pups are nut-brown at birth, 27 inches long and weigh between 13 and 15 pounds. The pups enter the water for the first time at the age of ten days, and are suckled for six months. They are very playful animals; they play with each other, and with the adults, and they seem to greatly enjoy chasing bubbles which they blow from under the water.

The food of the California sea lion is comprised mainly of octopuses and squids; but fish are also taken. This sea

(Above)
The Californian sea lion is quite small and the largest males weigh no more than 440 pounds. They are easily trained and it is this species that appears in circuses.

(Right)
This family portrait emphasizes the difference in the appearance of southern sea lions according to age and sex. The bull may weigh up to half a ton.

Walruses, identifiable by their long tusks, live in the sea in enormous herds. They herd by sex—males on one side, females and young on the other. In spring they haul out on the beaches and the males fight for the females. Pregnancy lasts a year, the pups being born shortly before the next mating.

Otaries are distinguished from seals by their little pointed ears, their relatively long necks and their mobile hind limbs. The ones in this picture—Cape fur seals—owe their name to their rich, glossy fur. This fur is greatly sought after by the fur trade.

lion swallows large quantities of stones, including sharp pieces of lava that can give rise to stomach upset. It is host to a great number of internal parasites, and also suffers from diseases of the main heart artery and inflammation of the lungs. Apart from man, the greatest enemies of the California sea lion are the killer whale and the shark. Present population is estimated at 50,000 in California, 20,000 in the Galapagos, and about 300 in Japan.

California sea lions are very popular in circuses and in zoological gardens especially the gentle females.

Their life span is from 12 to 14 years but there is a record of one animal that lived to the age of 30 years.

(Top)
When wet the California sea lion's coat looks black; but as soon as it begins to dry it is seen that it is light fawn.

(Above)
The otary's hind flippers are used only for steering. The animal oars itself along with its fore flippers.

California sea lion males, which are considerably larger than the females, keep constant watch over their harems. The pups are born in May and June and are suckled for six months. At birth, they weigh 13 pounds and are about two feet long. They are very playful and begin to paddle when only ten days old.

Steller's Sea Lion

Steller's sea lion *(Eumetopias jubata),* **also known as the northern sea lion, is a very large species.**

Males can reach a length of 12 feet and can weigh nearly a ton. An animal of this size will measure ten feet in body circumference. Females are much smaller, up to eight feet in length and 660 pounds in weight.

This species has a relatively long head and neck. The eyes are large and expressive; the ears are hollow tubes. On the upper lip, there are about 30 whitish flexible whiskers that sometimes reach a length of 17 inches.

Although the flippers can serve as legs, they are better adapted for movement in the water than on land. They are covered by thick granular skin. The coat is short, hard and glossy, with hairs of uniform length. Adult males vary from black to reddish-brown, and all shades of gray, with considerable mottling. Adult females are almost always light brown while the pups have bluish-gray fur.

Steller's sea lion is found over the whole of the North Pacific, from the coast of California to Japan, including the Aleutian Islands, the Sea of Okhotsk, the Kuril Islands, Kamchatka, Sakhalin and Hokkaido. It is also found as far south as Santa Barbara Island, opposite Los Angeles.

Several times a year, these sea lions undertake considerable migrations about which little is known. Adults, especially those from the Aleutians, travel northwards in summer as far as the Bering Strait. During the summer, there is not a single old male to be seen on the entire coast of California. These sea lions, like most pinnipeds, are thought to prefer colder waters and to follow the movement of the ice floes.

About three-quarters of an hour's journey from San Francisco, there is a great sea cliff overhanging three rocks about 500 feet below. The place is a great tourist attraction because visitors standing on the cliff top can look down and see about 60 Steller's sea lions on the rocks, stretched out on ledges and between fissures. Grouped in ones and twos and more, they are in the charge of a gigantic bull stationed on the highest pinnacle. Occasionally, the majestic leader of this herd inflates his sturdy graceful neck and barks.

On the rocks, the sea lions sleep curled up like dogs, with their muzzles resting against stomach or flank.

During the breeding season, Steller's sea lions gather together in large herds. In California, the season lasts from May to August, in Alaska, from June to October. The males are the first to arrive at the rookeries, followed a few days later by the females.

The arrival of the females triggers off fierce outbreaks of fighting among the bulls. Such battles can last for several days, ending, only when one of the

In winter Steller's sea lions are found less than an hour's journey from San Francisco; but in summer they travel as far north as the Bering Strait.

combatants is exhausted, in an armistice rather than a peace. Battle is resumed as soon as the exhausted animal has recovered his strength. Sometimes two males tire each other to such an extent that they have to leave the battleground together. When this happens, a third male usually moves in to display his strength.

Because of delayed implantation, pregnancy in this species lasts a year so the bulls fight their ferocious battles over females about to give birth to their young. Virgin females mate with young bulls.

Once the harems are established, the cows give birth to their pups, which the bulls help to rear. At first, the pups show a marked dislike for the water, but their parents coax them in and teach them to swim, and soon they are playing happily in it.

During the breeding season bulls eat nothing and cows hardly anything. Occasionally, a female will go into the water to hunt, but sea lion cows in general are most reluctant to leave their young unattended, and do so only when danger threatens. If an adult cow is not pregnant, or if she has lost her pup of the year, she will suckle her young of the previous year despite the fact that it has been so long weaned.

Steller's bulls are mature at five years, but are not able to form harems until they are about ten years old. Females are mature at three years. Pups are weaned at the age of three months, by which time they are able to follow the adults anywhere. The herds spend the rest of the year at sea, wandering and hunting fish, molluscs and crustaceans. As some of their prey species have commercial value—for example, herring and salmon—fishermen regard sea lions as competitors.

Steller's sea lions were once plentiful along the California coast and were much exploited for their fat, from which thousands of barrels of oil were extracted each year. It takes the blubber of two or three sea lions to produce one barrel of oil so it is not difficult to imagine in what vast numbers animals were killed. When the decline in numbers became obvious, hunters confined themselves to killing males. They also began to use guns instead of spears, thus avoiding the cruel killing methods of the past. The sea lion's skin, formerly of no value, is now used in making glue.

On the coast of Siberia, Kamchatka and Sakhalin, Steller's sea lions are hunted during the summer, when they follow the migrating salmon into the rivers and bays of northern Asia. The local fishermen shut off parts of the rivers and bays with nets that let the fish through, but bar the passage of the sea lions which are caught in the mesh and drown.

Although Steller's sea lion can live in captivity, it is only rarely seen in zoological gardens because of its uncertain temper. Average life span is about 17 years. Man is the main enemy. The present world population of Steller's sea lions is estimated at 240,000 to 300,000.

Steller's sea lion is so called because of the mane on the bull's neck. Males can weigh up to a ton, but females no more than 660 pounds.

Alaskan Fur Seal
(*Pribilof fur seal*)

Unlike the sea lions, whose coarse hair is low quality fur, the fur seals, known as *Arctocephalinae*, **have a dense high quality under-fur which they retain throughout life.**

The Alaskan fur seal (*Callorhinus ursinus*) is much smaller than Steller's sea lion, the males reaching a length of seven feet and a weight of up to 660 pounds, while females do not exceed six feet and 330 pounds.

This seal is slim-bodied but strong. Its head is bigger and more tapered than that of other seals. It has a short, well-defined neck and a short tail. The mouth is small, the nostrils mere slits. The eyes are large, dark and expressive. The upper lip has 20 stiff whiskers about six inches in length.

The coat of the fur seal is valuable. Shiny, silky guard hairs cover the soft delicate woolly under-fur. The predominant tint is dark brown, almost black, with some white patches; the under parts are paler. Adult females are silvery gray. Pups look even whiter because of the light tips of their hair.

Alaskan fur seals, during migration, cover more ocean than any other pinniped. They cover the entire northern hemisphere, but their breeding stations are limited to the Pribilof and Commander Islands, and a few islands in the Bering Sea.

After the breeding season, the seals migrate from these stations in three main directions. Most of them, about four fifths, travel down the California coast as far as San Diego. Another group heads towards Japan. A third migrates through the North Pacific to the Aleutians. The seals travel in small groups of about 15, and rarely more than 50 miles from land.

At the breeding stations, adult males occupy the same territory year after year. They arrive on station at the end of May. From then on, there is much noise and fighting among territorial bulls defending their frontiers, or over the selection and defining of new territories. The cows arrive a month later and harems are quickly set up, each composed of a bull and 50 or more females.

Pregnancy in this species lasts from 11 to 12 months, and the cows give birth to their pup a few days after they join the bulls. Occasionally, a cow has twins. The pups are about 27 inches long, weigh about 13 pounds, and are born

Fur seals have a short, dense, lustrous coat which resembles velvet and is much sought after by the fur trade. This picture shows the Pribilof fur seals.

with their eyes open. They are born with short crisp black fur which is soon moulted and replaced by a coat of long gray hair.

The cow stays with her pup constantly for the first week of its life. After that, she begins to hunt and spends longer and longer periods in the sea each day. At the age of a month, the pups are active, playing and paddling all day. Now they suckle their mother only once a week, but the hungry gap is compensated for by the quantity of milk at the weekly meal—about four quarts at one time.

Cow fur seals are mature at three years old and give birth to their first pup at the age of four years. Bulls are mature at five or six years, but do not begin to breed until the age of eight years. They are in their prime at 15 years old, and it is not until then that they begin to set up harems. Between the ages of eight and fifteen, they mate with virgin females or females too young to join a harem.

Nowadays, much more is known, and accurately known, about the diet of fur seals. Modern techniques of stomach analysis provide a fairly precise picture of what they eat and how much of each item they eat. Research has shown that their food consists of:

Lantern fish (*Myctophidae*)	60%
Cephalopods	27%
Anchovies	8%
Salmon	3%
Mackerel and other fish	2%

Pribilof fur seals were once very numerous. By 1890, the annual total of seals killed at sea had reached 62,000. This was heavy exploitation but the real massacres began with the discovery of their breeding grounds. Any animal whose breeding stations are known, and which is tied to them for a known period, becomes extremely vulnerable. Annual uncontrolled slaughter threatened the fur seal with annihilation. Now, action has been taken by the countries ringing the Polar seas—the United States, Canada, the U.S.S.R. and Japan. Protection halted, and has now reversed, the trend towards extinction.

Nowadays, no one can land on the Pribilof Islands, except in case of emergency, without express Government permission. As a result of this, the population of fur seals, down to 130,000 in 1900, is now 1½ million. The species

is now in such a strong position that controlled hunting is permitted. The season begins on 20th June and lasts for five weeks. Only young animals under three years old can be killed.

Cape Fur Seal

The Cape fur seal (*Arctocephalinae pusillus*) **is found in the southern hemisphere where there are six species.**

They differ hardly at all from each other except that they live in different places, and they are:

The Cape fur seal
(*Arctocephalinae pusillus*)
The New Zealand fur seal
(*Arctocephalinae forsteri*)
The Australian fur seal
(*Arctocephalinae doriferus*)
The Kerguelen fur seal
(*Arctocephalinae tropicalis*)
The Tasmanian fur seal
(*Arctocephalinae tasmanius*)
The southern fur seal
(*Arctocephalinae australis*)

Lastly, there is a colony of under 500 Guadalupe fur seals (*Arctocephalinae philippii*) found round Guadalupe, the only surviving *Arctocephalinae* in the northern hemisphere. At one time, there

must have been millions of these seals in the world but they were ruthlessly exploited by nineteenth century sealers who, in destroying their own livelihood, almost wiped out the species.

The Cape fur seal is slightly larger than the Pribilof fur seal, with a higher forehead and a more pronounced muzzle. The biggest males reach a length of eight feet with a weight range of 600 to 770 pounds, according to season. Females are much smaller, up to six feet in length. They weigh up to 260 pounds. Although this seal's coat is less dense and of lower quality than that of the Pribilof fur seal, it is still much in demand. It is brown, black or gray, and quite often a mixture of all three. Over-hunting has seriously reduced the Cape seal population, which is now estimated to be between 500,000 and 900,000. The disparity in these estimates is explained by the fact that there is great annual variation in the number of pups born and in the rate of pup mortality.

Although this species undertakes no long regular migrations, it moves over a wide area of sea in search of food and is often sighted 100 miles or more from land. Between breeding seasons, bull seals will spend two or three weeks at a time on feeding expeditions. The main diet of the Cape fur seal is fish, squids, rock

The coat of the Cape fur seal is not as beautiful as that of the Pribilof fur seal, but is still much in demand. Cape fur seals are also hunted for their fat.

lobsters and some crustaceans.

The breeding season is in November. The bulls arrive first at the rookeries and select their territory. Harems are set up as soon as the females arrive, a harem consisting of five to ten cows.

Soon after arrival, the cows give birth to their pups. Single pups are usual. At birth, the pup weighs 15 pounds, measures 27 inches in length, and has all its milk teeth. Its birth coat is a short crumpled down which it loses at the age of four or five months. This is replaced by an olive-green and white coat which it retains for a few months. At a year old, the pup moults into a coat of silvery gray.

The cows suckle their young ashore for about ten months, leaving them for periods of a few days or a week at a time to hunt for food. This long nursing period prevents the cows from making any long journeys. This means that herds of fur seals seen near the coast usually consist of cows and their young. Stones are often found in the stomachs of these seals—as they are in other species—irrespective of age or of sex.

Cape fur seal females are mature at two years old, males at three years. The life span is about 20 years. Fur seals are hunted for their fat and for their skins. In Uruguay, the fat is made into oil which is very rich in vitamins; it is taken, as a diet supplement, by people suffering from tuberculosis.

Cape fur seals live in the southern hemisphere. They do not travel far from their birthplace, and gather together in November to mate and give birth to their young.

Sirenians

These are the only sea mammals that live entirely on vegetable matter. They have weak eyesight but good hearing. The name of the order is derived from the sirens of Greek mythology.

The name of this order *(Sirenia)* **is derived from the sirens of Greek mythology who lured unwary mariners to destruction by their sweet seductive songs.**

Orpheus saved his Argonauts by singing so beautifully himself that none of his crew wanted to listen to the song of the sirens. Odysseus stuffed his crew's ears with wax and lashed himself to the mast until he was out of hearing.

But the sirens of the sea—the real ones, known as manatees and dugongs—are quite unlike the nymphs of Greek mythology except for their breasts which bear a crude similarity to the human female's. In shallow water, the animals rest with their heads and backs above the surface while holding their young to their breasts. What could look more like mermaids to a tired-eyed, homesick sailor?

Unlike the seals, walruses and sea lions, the sirenians are vegetarians, eating marine plants, algae and seaweed. They are the only aquatic mammals that live entirely on vegetable matter.

The sirenians have small heads and massive spindle-shaped bodies, ending in horizontal paddles. The tail paddle is not formed by the fusion of hind limbs; these have completely disappeared. The fore limbs have become flippers, with rudimentary nails on the finger tips, except in a South American species which has none. The upper lip, which bristles with whiskers, is remarkably developed and overhangs the lower.

The teeth grow constantly throughout the animal's lifetime. The molars wear out, disappear and are replaced, as in the elephant, by new ones. The horny plate

Sirenians are aquatic mammals that bear little resemblance to the seductive sirens of mythology. The one in this picture lives in fresh water; it is a manatee.

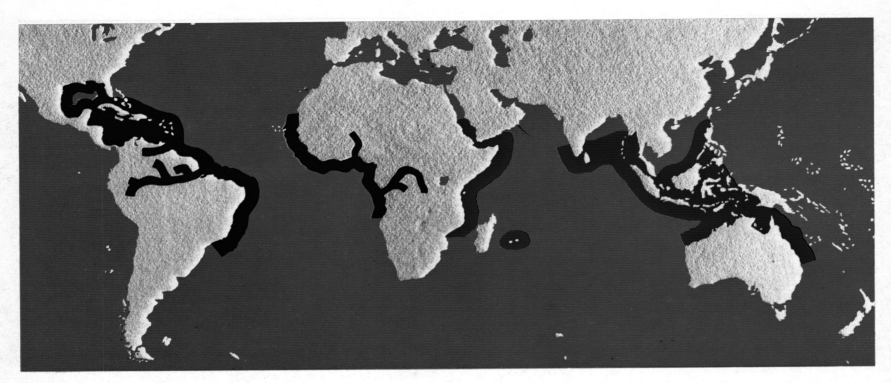

ORDER OF SIRENIANS

Family	Genus
Trichechidae	*Trichechus*
Dugongidae or Halicoridae	*Dugong*

in the mouth plays a greater part than the teeth in the grinding of food. There is a small ear hole, but no external ear. The nostrils are situated on top of the nose and can be closed at will.

Sirenians have weak eyesight, but good hearing.

Sirenians uproot their food by blows from the upper lip. The bristles on the lip help them to sort out and collect seaweeds. Their sense of smell must be extremely well developed for this method of selection.

Sirenians prefer shallow water, and are therefore frequently found in river estuaries. Some of them will travel upstream into lakes. They live in pairs or small herds and appear to be strictly monogamous. Although lacking in the agility of the seals, sirenians can swim and dive with the greatest of ease, but they avoid deep water. The young are born under water, then brought to the surface by the mother. On land, sirenians are incapable of coordinating their movements and, stranded, are condemned to a slow death, however near the water they may be lying.

Trichechidae

The animals of this family have the tail fin shaped like a rounded paddle. The fore limbs have four flat nails on the fingers. There are six neck bones instead of the seven usual in mammals. The eye glands emit a jelly-like secretion; hence the origin of the idea that the sirenians could weep. In each half of the jaw, the *Trichechidae* have five or six teeth, rarely eight, which are regularly renewed so that the animal can produce sixty teeth in its lifetime.

Florida Manatee

The Florida manatee (*Trichechus manatus*) **is the best known and the most studied member of the family.** It is found on the west coast of Florida, in the Caribbean and on the west coast of South America, mostly in estuaries where sea water and fresh water meet. But it will readily travel a long way upstream and, during periods of flooding, will live in lakes and flood plains.

This species can grow to a length of 15 feet and can reach a weight of over 1,300 pounds. Most specimens, however, are between 8 feet and 13 feet in length, and weigh between 300 and 800 pounds. The skin is two inches thick and varies from gray to black.

The upper lip is cleft and the parts can move independently. They are highly sensitive and act as organs of touch. The lungs are three feet long, taking in a vast quantity of air. This explains the manatee's ability to stay under water, feeding, for up to 15 minutes at a time. The intestine is more than 100 feet long.

Like other sirenians, the Florida manatee lives exclusively on vegetable matter. The river beds are rich in water plants of many kinds, so it does not have to look far for its food. It eats so much at a time that it fills its stomach and intestine completely. After feeding, it remains motionless in the shallows, and spends most of the day dozing, raising its head above the surface from time to time to breathe.

Female manatees give birth to a single calf after a gestation period of 152 to 180 days. The calf is born under water, then immediately brought to the surface by its mother. It is suckled for a period of eighteen months, always under water. Both parents care for it up to the age of two years.

In Florida, this manatee is protected by law. Any person killing one is fined 500 dollars or sent to prison. Apart from man, the manatee's only enemies are sharks and alligators, which prey mainly on very young calves.

The Amazonian manatee (*Trichechus inunguis*) is similar to the Florida manatee, but is found only in fresh water, on the north-east coast of South America and in the Amazon and Orinoco Basins.

(Top)
Sirenians live in the tropics, along the coasts and in rivers. Manatees live in America and Africa (area shaded blue) and dugongs in the East (area shaded red).

(Right)
The manatee has tiny eyes and its sight is very poor. It lives in shallow waters, surfacing every ten minutes to breathe.

Dugongidae

The sirenians of this group have the normal seven neck bones. All the dugongs belong to a single species, not three as was once thought by zoologists.

Class	**Mammalia**
Order	**Sirenia**
Family	**Dugongidae**

The *Dugongidae,* **also named** *Halicoridae* **can be recognized by their notched tail fin.**

Their bodies are more streamlined than those of the manatees and their fore fins have no claws. The dugong is the only surviving member of this family. The other, Steller's sea cow, which was found in the Bering Sea, was exterminated by man in the second half of the eighteenth century, probably by 1768.

Dugong

The dugong *(Dugong dugong),* **familiar to the ancient Chinese and Arabs, was discovered by Europeans only at the beginning of the nineteenth century.**

Like the manatee, it is a vegetarian, feeding mainly on seaweed and grazing on the sea bottom, as cattle do on land. For this reason, dugongs are often referred to as sea cows.

At one time, three species of dugong were recognized by zoologists. Today, however, the general consensus of opinion is that they all belong to the present species.

The neck of the dugong is so short that its head appears to be an extension of its spindle-shaped body. Length varies from eight feet to ten feet, and weight from 330 to 550 pounds.

The snout is short and fat, strongly muscled and layered with blubber. The lip is covered with soft skin. The mouth hangs obliquely at the front and looks as though it were separated from the head, thus giving the animal a distorted profile. The nostrils, situated on the upper side of the snout, are crescent shaped slits set close together. The eyes are lidless slits, but have a nictitating— or winking—membrane that can be closed by skin contraction. The ear holes are minute openings.

The fins are hairless. The body hairs

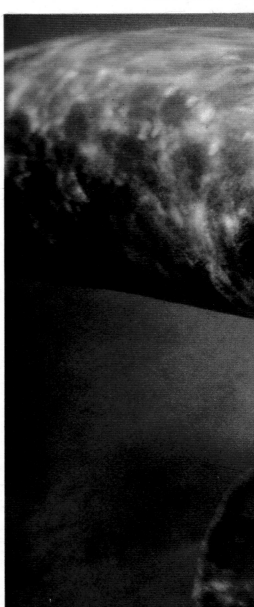

(Above and top, right)
The manatee's tail fin is shaped like a rounded paddle. Its fore limbs form fins. The hind limbs have completely disappeared.

(Right)
The manatee gives birth to a single calf under water. The calf weighs 44 pounds at birth; it is suckled for 18 months and remains with its parents for two years.

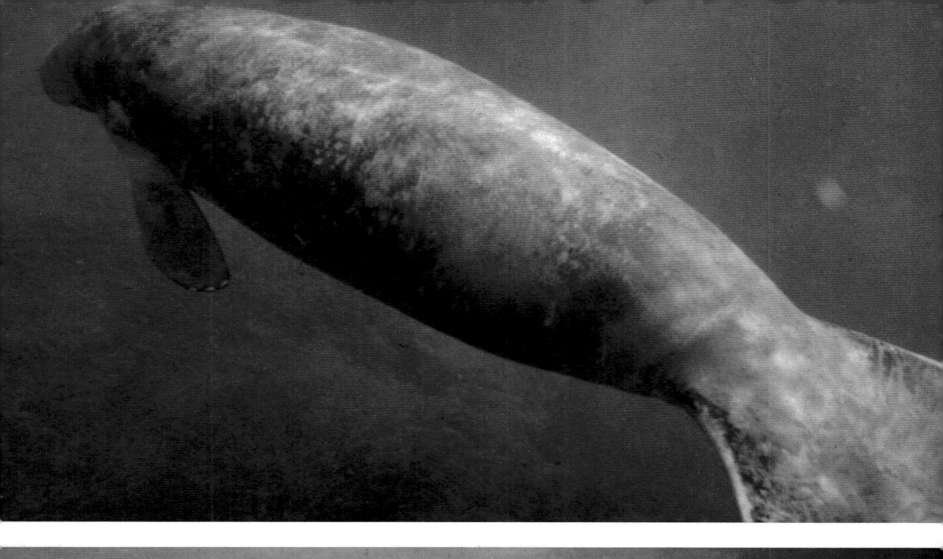

are sparse, short, fine and stiff. Those on the upper lip form vibrissae.

Dugongs have only two kinds of teeth—incisors and molars, all of them without roots. Over the years, most of the incisors are shed. In females, these are short, rounded and sharp; in males, they are stronger and triangular in shape. The animals have no canine teeth but, in males, two of the incisors project from their mouth to form tusks up to ten inches long. Most of their length is concealed in the mouth, with only an inch or so of tusk protruding.

The dugong is common along the coasts of the Indian Ocean, in the Red Sea, on the East African coast and around the Islands of the Bay of Bengal—also in the Malayan Archipelago, the Molucca Islands, the Philippines, New Guinea and the Australian coast, north of the 25th Parallel. It lives in the sea, preferably near river estuaries. (But the dugong does not live in the rivers themselves.) It stays near the coast and does not venture out to sea beyond the beds of vegetation where it feeds.

The dugong favours shallow, sunlit coves where the water plants are plentiful. Every minute or so, it surfaces to breathe and then lets itself sink placidly to the bottom once more.

Groups of dugongs, even small ones, are rare. Couples are usual, or two adults with a calf. So long as there is plenty of food, the animals lead remarkably settled lives, moving only when they have grazed an area clean. In winter, however, they usually migrate northwards.

Not a great deal is known about dugongs. They appear to have no set mating season. Gestation is thought to last 11 months, and the females have a single calf each year.

It is known that the female dugong is a good mother who looks after her calf with great care, and sometimes carries it on her back. When suckling her calf, the mother holds it to her breast with a flipper. The suckling period is about a year.

Fishermen hunt the dugong relentlessly for its fat, flesh, oil, and certain body parts to which they attribute therapeutic and other values.

In Indonesia, necklaces made from dugong teeth are considered to have many virtues and mysterious powers. The superstitious believe that cigarette holders made from the tusks of male dugongs will protect the owners against poisoning and even bullets. In Madagascar, the fat from the head is used to cure migraines. The harder fat is used as a laxative.

The dugong population is still declining and, if not given protection, the species may become extinct.

(Left)
The manatee is exclusively herbivorous, and eats water plants in vast quantities. When it has eaten its fill, it spends most of its time dozing until it is hungry again.

Although it has no eyelids, the dugong can close its eyes by contracting the skin of its forehead. Its nostrils are situated on the top of its snout.

55

Cetaceans

The animals of this group are the most perfectly adapted of all mammals to life in the water. Apart from the streamlining of their bodies, they have developed fins like fish and do in fact resemble large fish. They are all carnivores.

Class	**Mammalia**
Order	**Cetacea**

Like all mammals, the cetaceans are warm-blooded, breathe atmospheric air and suckle their young. Of all the marine mammals, they are the most completely adapted to life in the water.

Only the ocean can provide them with their food and habitat. They die if stranded in shallow water or ashore.

The body of the cetaceans is massive, tapered, and perfectly streamlined. The enormous head tapers, fish-like, into the massive trunk. They are fish-shaped mammals—they even have an adipose dorsal fin to heighten the resemblance. But here the resemblance to the fishes ends; in fish, the tail fin is always vertical, in the cetaceans, it is always horizontal.

The fore fins of the cetaceans enclose arm, forearm and finger bones, three to five in number, with up to fourteen joints, or phalanges. The mammary glands are at the rear end of the body. The mouth is wide and contains a great number of horny teeth or plates, known as baleen. The skin is fine, soft, velvety and oily, with a thick layer of blubber underneath.

The tongue is highly developed but there are no salivary glands. The stomach is divided into several compartments, varying from four to 14 according to species.

The respiratory organs are unusual. The nose, which has no sense of smell, has become a blowhole—a simple air passage leading vertically from the nasal cavity to the top of the head. In other words, the windpipe passes right through the throat, dividing the gullet in two.

None of the sense organs is very highly developed. The eyes are small; the ears hardly visible from the outside. In the water, they seem to hear well enough; out of it, they hear very poorly or not at all. But cetaceans often have good vision.

The horizontal tail fin propels the animal through the water, and enables it to dive and surface at will. The pectoral fins are used more as stabilizers.

Cetaceans carry out regular migrations, returning every year to the same place to give birth to their young. They are sociable animals. In areas where food is plentiful, several species can be found together mixing, sometimes in large groups. It would appear that migrating herds are often composed of different species, mostly females accompanied by their young, with an escort of a few males.

All cetaceans are agile and lively in their movements. They can swim with the greatest of agility and without apparent effort. The strength of their tail fin allows them, despite their great weight, to surface rapidly and even to leap out of the water.

When a cetacean surfaces, it expels jets of warm, damp air through its blowhole. When the surrounding temperature is low, the mist from the blowhole condenses and looks like a spout of water. After the first noisy blow, the animal rapidly expels all the stale air from its lungs, then takes a deep breath before diving again. It can remain under water, without breathing, for ten to 20 minutes, and sometimes even longer. A harpooned bottle-nosed whale has been known to spend two hours under water.

The volume of the lungs in cetaceans, compared with their body volume, is no greater than in man. In right whales, it is, in fact, only half the comparative volume.

The lungs are, in great part, formed of an elastic tissue that allows rapid ventilation. The distribution of the respira-

Suborder	Family	Genus
Mysteceti	**Balaenidae**	*Neobalaena, Eubalaena, Balaena*
	Balaenopteridae	*Sibbaldus, Megaptera, Balaenoptera*
	Eschrichtidae or Rachianechtidae	*Eschrichtius*
	Phocaenidae	*Neophocaena, Phocaena*
	Delphinidae	*Lissodelphis, Globicephala, Orcaella, Pseudorca, Orcinus, Cephalorbynchus, Lagenorhynchus, Tursiops, Grampus, Delphinus, Prodelphinus, Sotalia, Steno*
Odontoceti	**Delphinapteridae**	*Monodon, Delphinapterus*
	Physeteridae	*Kogia, Physeter*
	Ziphiidae	*Hyperoodon, Tasmacetus, Ziphius Mesoplodon*
	Platanistidae	*Stenodelphis, Lipotes, Inia, Platanista*

Distribution of balaenidae (shown in green). Decimated by intensive hunting, whales have become so rare that good records are exceptional.

(Right)
The manatee's upper lip is split lengthwise and the halves act independently.

tory capillaries is unusual and highly effective. Oxygen is carried quickly to the tissues where it is rapidly fixed by the high number of red corpuscles in the blood.

The rorqual, or finback whale, can dive to 650 feet and return to the surface without being upset by the sudden release of nitrogen gases which dissolve at high pressure. Thus, it avoids "bends" or "diver's sickness" which is a well-known hazard in man. Everything about the cetaceans is designed to prevent this, including slow surfacing, punctuated by stages of decompression. Finally, the "wonderful plexus" of the cetacean—its network of nerves, blood vessels, tissue—is designed to regulate the temperature of the flippers and slow down the flow of blood to certain areas, allowing the animal to have a reserve of blood rich in oxygen in vital parts of its body.

The sounds uttered by cetaceans have given rise to much speculation among zoologists. The fact that the animals have a glottis or voice box proves that they do have a voice, even though it is rarely heard. Precise experiments have shown that dolphins are able to emit and detect a variety of sounds in the audible and ultrasonic ranges. The extent to which they use echo location, as bats do, is still being investigated.

All cetaceans are carnivorous, probably eating vegetable matter by accident or when they have no choice. Odontoceti are all predators, or even cannibals; but the Mysteceti consume very small animals—fish, crustaceans, molluscs, jellyfish. It is easy to imagine the enormous quantity of food required by these gigantic animals. The right whale, a giant of the family, eats several million, or even several thousand million, small marine animals every day.

Very little is known about the breeding of these animals, mainly because they are so difficult to observe. Some species, like dolphins, have been more closely studied because they can be kept in captivity. In the case of the others, zoologists have had to be satisfied with the study of embryos found in specimens killed by whalers.

The gestation period varies from six to 20 months according to species, and a single calf is usual. A new born calf, which measures up to a quarter or even a third the length of its mother, is surprisingly precocious. A blue whale is nearly 23 feet long at birth, and weighs 4,400 pounds. Like all cetacean calves, it can swim immediately after birth and can, without instruction, suckle its mother.

In the Mysteceti, the calves are born in warm waters, and are nursed for several months. The mother surfaces and turns on her side, so that the calf is able to take hold of her teat. As soon as the calf touches a teat, the milk spurts out under pressure. There are two breasts, not easily seen, each with one teat. The very rich and fatty milk has the consistency of thick cream.

Cetaceans have many enemies, especially sharks and killer whales which prey on the calves and even attack adults. But the most dangerous enemy of all is man who has hunted them since the fourteenth century.

Whaling today is big business despite the fact that certain countries have opted out almost entirely. Indeed, the United States and Britain have virtually ceased hunting whales.

Nowadays, special ships, known as factory ships, are used, the whole animal being processed at sea.

Whaling is, today, controlled to some extent by international agreement intended to prevent the total extinction of these giant mammals of the sea.

(Pages 58–59)
Cetaceans are the mammals that are best adapted to aquatic life. The adipose fin on the back accentuates their resemblance to fish.

(Left)
Cetaceans, especially whales, contain vast quantities of meat and, more particularly, fat and oil. Man has hunted them since the fourteenth century.

(Above)
Cetaceans are warm-blooded animals with lungs. They have to surface from time to time to breathe.

Mysteceti

The cetaceans of this suborder, which includes the right whales and rorquals, have whalebone plates instead of teeth.

These horny plates, known as baleen, are situated on either side of the upper jaw. They are triangular or square in section, and number up to 400. They are longest and set closest together in the middle of the jaw. When the animal closes its mouth, the upper jaw fits into the lower. The baleen plates, which have a fringed edge, seal the mouth perfectly and act like a sieve which traps the minutest prey. The jaws of the animals in this group are enormous in relation to the size of the head. They are lengthened like beaks and concave like bows. The tongue is very large and immovable. The Mysteceti are extremely large animals, measuring up to 110 feet in length and weighing from 20 to 130 tons. They are the largest living animals and so far as one can tell, in the present state of our knowledge, they are the largest that have ever lived.

They eat fish, molluscs, crustaceans, jelly-fish and other small marine organisms: but their special food is plankton. They feed literally by swimming along with their mouths open. They fill their mouths with water and close their jaws.

The vertical sheets of whalebone form a grille which allows the water to be expelled, retaining the smallest prey.

Balaenidae

This is the family of the right whales and their name means exactly that. They are the _true_ whales.

Distinguishing characteristics of this family are:

1. Absence of a dorsal fin.
2. Absence of guttural and ventral grooves, found in the other two families of Mysteceti.
3. A concave upper jaw.
4. Long narrow baleen plates.
5. Neck bones all joined together.
6. Upper and lower jaws never in contact, but always with a large free space between.

Greenland Right Whale

The Greenland right whale (_Balaena mysticetus_) **measures from 50 to 65 feet in length, about a third of which is the massive head. The mouth is 16 to 20 feet long and eight feet wide. The fluked tail can reach a width of 20 to 26 feet.**

Compared with rorquals the right whale is a massive bulky animal. Its body is thick-set and rounded. Around the blowholes the head looks swollen. The blowholes are two narrow slits about 18 inches long and situated about ten feet from the point of the snout. The eyes, which are hardly bigger than those of a walrus, are placed where the lower jaw joins the skull. The ears are slightly recessed. The plates of baleen, 300 to 360 on each side of the mouth, can reach over 13 feet in length and weigh seven pounds each. The enormous tongue is soft; the lower lips are as long as the head, and can be seven feet thick.

The hairless skin of the Greenland whale is strong and supple and feels like oiled leather. The underlying blubber is from eight to 18 inches thick. The general shade is black, except for the throat and chin which are pale cream. Females are usually bigger and fatter than males. Their mammary glands are the size of a cow's udder, and pale.

As its name suggests, the Greenland right whale is found in the seas around the North Pole. It is no longer found in the North Atlantic or Pacific or in the European part of the Arctic Ocean. Nowadays, it is to be seen only west of Canada, in the Bering Sea, Baffin Bay and the far North of Hudson Bay. Its movements are dictated by the ice. It moves south with the advancing ice, and north as the ice fields melt. In the Davis Strait, it never goes further south than 65° North.

Right whales are sociable animals, found usually in small groups of three or four, but in larger herds when on migration. Such herds are always made up of animals of the same age.

When undisturbed, right whales surface every ten to 15 minutes. They stay up from one to three minutes, during which time they breathe four to six times. Their spout—columns of air saturated with water which rise from their blowholes—can reach a height of 14 feet and is visible from a long way off. Although whales are not vocal, it has now been established that they can utter certain sounds.

The main food of this whale is krill, the plankton of the northern seas, which is very abundant in the areas they frequent. They also eat crustaceans and fish, provided they are very small.

The mating season is at the end of summer. Pregnancy lasts about ten months. As a rule, the female gives

Thanks to their thick layer of blubber, cetaceans can float easily. This picture shows a California gray whale.

Cetaceans are not very prolific. They usually
have a single calf, rarely two, born under
water. The mother suckles its calf and cares
for it lovingly.

63

birth to a single calf, but rare cases of twins have been reported. The calf measures between 12 and 18 feet at birth, and is nursed for a year, during which time it grows rapidly. By the time it is weaned, the calf measures about 20 feet long, 13 feet in circumference and weighs about 13,200 pounds. The female whale is a very good mother and will defend her calf against all enemies.

The right whale was once heavily exploited by whalers. The body of a fully grown adult provided from 12,000 to 16,000 quarts of oil, and 1,500 to 2,200 pounds of baleen or whalebone. This whalebone was once used in the manufacture of corsets.

Where it succeeds in escaping man, the right whale can live to an advanced age. Man, however, isn't its only enemy. It sometimes falls a prey to the killer whale. It is also host to many parasites, especially small crustaceans called "whale lice" which live on its back in hundreds of thousands. The whale lice, in turn, afford an excellent habitat for algae, so that the whale literally carries on its back a whole world of plants and animals.

Balaenopteridae

The *Balaenopteridae* or rorquals are distinguished from right whales by the

(Top)
The cetacean's tail fin propels it along. It is so powerful that the whale is able to leap right out of the water.

(Above)
The nose of cetaceans is a simple passage which opens at the top of the head through an orifice called the blowhole. This is not used for smelling.

presence of deep lengthwise parallel grooves on the throat, breast, and part of the abdomen. Their bodies are less bulky, and their heads less massive. The upper jaw is not arched. The baleen is shorter and wider.

Blue Whale

The blue whale (*Sibbaldus musculus*) **is the largest mammal the world has ever known.**

It measures from 65 to 100 feet in length but some specimens reach a length of 110 feet. Its pectoral fins are 13 feet long. A very large blue whale can top 130 tons in weight.

The predominant shade is dark slate blue, with white on the breast, the abdomen and the underside of the fins. The dorsal fin, which is situated far back on the body, is very small. On the underside of the body, there are about 100 deep grooves in the skin, stretching along half its length.

This whale is found mostly in the Antarctic. In winter, it travels northwards as far as the coast of Africa, but it avoids tropical seas. A few blue whales are also found in the northern hemisphere, around Greenland.

In the southern hemisphere, the blue whale mates in July. The period of

(*Top*)
Cetaceans are sociable animals which undertake periodic migrations. The herds, of varying sizes, are composed mainly of females and juveniles.

(*Above*)
Cetaceans have smooth skins which help them when swimming. Their layer of blubber decreases their specific gravity. The tail fin is horizontal—not vertical, as in fishes.

65

gestation is from ten to 11 months. One calf is usual. It measures 23 feet long at birth, and is able to swim, dive, and suckle under water from the start. By the end of six months, it has doubled in size and is able to eat the plankton and shrimps which are abundant in parts of the Antarctic.

Unlike the right whale, the blue can move at great speed—up to 15 knots when being pursued. Its speed saved it in the old days, when no long boat could catch it. But it cannot escape modern vessels equipped with harpoon guns.

It is estimated that, since 1900, 330,000 blue whales have been killed by whalers, and it is thought that fewer than 1,000 now exist. Although now protected, the number left may be too few to allow the species to recover. It may be below what is known as the threshold of survival.

Humpback Whale

The humpback whale (*Megaptera novaeangliae*) **is about 50 feet long and weighs about 30 tons. This is a thick-set whale, with a sharply convex back and long pectoral fins about a third the length of its body.**

The pectoral fins are white. There are between ten and 25 furrows on the neck and underside of the body. The humpback whale is deep black above and whitish underneath.

This is the whale most frequently seen because it lives in coastal waters and shallow bays as well as in the open sea. It is known for its regular migrations. Humpbacks, in southern waters, migrate in autumn to the coast of Africa, as far as the Congo and Madagascar. Farther east, they travel to Australia and New Zealand. In spring, the animals return to the Antarctic. Recent research has established that each herd follows a traditional route, moving to a well defined area in the tropics, and returning to an equally well defined area in the Antarctic.

In the northern hemisphere, their migrations have not been so closely studied and are not so well understood. There is one route from the Canaries to Spitsbergen, another from the Mexican coast to the Bering Sea, another from the Antilles to Baffin Bay, and one from the Marianas to Kamchatka.

It is unlikely that the whales of the northern hemisphere ever come into contact with those from Antarctica.

The humpback is a gregarious animal, and sometimes forms large herds. The humpback whale swims slowly. However, it often leaps out of the water, displaying its tail fin. It would appear that the humpback is of an extremely happy disposition. Many people believe that it leaps out of the water from sheer *joie de vivre*.

The gestation period is probably 12 months. The calf, which is born tail first, measures about 13 feet in length

and weighs 2,900 pounds. The mother suckles it for between ten and 11 months, and displays all the tenderness characteristic of cetaceans.

Forty years ago, the population of humpbacks was estimated at 22,000. It is now thought that there are fewer than 3,000 in the Antarctic, and about 5,000 in the North Pacific. Having reached such a dangerous figure, the species is now protected.

Common Rorqual (*Balaenoptera Physalus*)

The common rorqual, also known as the finback whale, is smaller and darker than the blue whale, and of much more slender build.

It can measure up to 80 feet in length, but usually ranges between 60 and 67 feet. The skin is gray on the back; white on the underside. The left side of the jaw is often darker than the right side. There are about 90 grooves on the underside, the tips of which are bluish black. This species is particularly abundant in the Antarctic during the summer, but is found in every ocean. It can move at high speed. In general habits it is little different from other Mysteceti, except that it eats fish—notably herrings and haddocks—besides plankton and crus-

Right whales, whose baleen provided the whalebone for corsets, are no longer hunted. Modern whalers hunt rorquals. This giant animal is a blue whale.

The common rorqual can swim at high speed. Growing up to 80 feet in length, it is the species most hunted by whalers today.

taceans. When hunting fish, it ventures close to the shore and has been seen fishing in the Norwegian fjords.

The finback is the most hunted whale species today, and whalers have concentrated on it ever since the end of World War II. Their annual catch is about 25,000. In 1960, the size of the catch was limited by international agreement. But although herds of about 100 can still be seen, the finback is in danger of meeting the same fate as other whales, unless it is rigorously protected in certain areas.

Eschrichtidae

There is only one member in this family of baleen whales—the California gray whale (*Eschrichtius gibbosus*) **found near the American and Korean coasts.**

There are, at present two distinct groups of California gray whales. The first spends the summer in the Bering Sea, wintering in the Gulf of California. The second group spends the summer months in the Sea of Okhotsk in northeast Asia, and winters off South Korea.

The California gray whale can be recognized by the absence of a dorsal fin. In its place, there are ten nodules. The baleen blades are short and few in number. This species measures from 30 to 50 feet in length, and weighs between 25 and 35 tons. As in other whales, the females are usually larger than the males. There are three or four shallow grooves on the under side. The body is light or dark gray with many whitish patches, some of which are due to the absence of pigment, and others to the presence of parasites.

Like the right whale, the California gray whale moves slowly. It has a cruising speed of about four knots and a maximum speed, when pursued, of seven or eight knots. Its lack of speed, and the fact that its body floated when dead, made it a target for the old time whalers who could hunt it with a harpoon and then tow the body to the shore to be cut up. The species was decimated in the first half of the nineteenth century. But it was given full protection in 1938 and the population is slowly recovering.

Odontoceti

Unlike the Mysteceti, the whales of this group have teeth instead of baleen. The number of teeth varies from species to species—from two in Cuvier's whale up to 260 in the dolphin. This suborder contains the majority of cetaceans.

Hearing is the most highly developed sense and the animals react mainly to sound. They can hear and identify subtle sounds and are constantly uttering sounds themselves. The sounds they utter cover a wide range, from whistles audible to the human ear to the ultrasonic which the human ear cannot hear.

(Top left)
The humpback whale has very long pectoral fins. It lives in all the world's seas, sometimes in large herds.

(Top right)
The California gray whale's skin has white patches. There are few ventral grooves. The species is now fully protected.

These sounds fill two roles. They allow the animals to communicate with each other and they act as a sonar system—in other words, the animals are guided by echo location.

Bats use echo location. They send out sound waves which bounce back from any object ahead of them, thus registering the position. The dolphin operates in the same way in the water. When it is swimming towards an object, its head moves from side to side like a dog cocking its ears. These movements enable the dolphin to fix the origin of the echo and it navigates according to the intensity and location of the sound it receives.

The diversity of sounds produced allows for numerous combinations which can be said to make up a language or code. The frequency and pitch of the sound changes according to whether the animal is calling its calf, or warning it of the approach of danger, or the presence of prey.

The animals of this group are notable for having in their heads a mass of adipose tissue—variable in size, but generally round in form—which contains an oil reservoir, known as spermaceti. While the animal is alive, the spermaceti is liquid, but it solidifies to form a compact white mass after the animal is dead. The solidification is the result of the drop in body temperature. So spermaceti is always in solid form when it is collected by the whaler.

The fine wax extracted from spermaceti is used in the manufacture of perfumes and cosmetics. Its purpose in the living animal is not clear but, according to some writers, the spermaceti can detect variations in pressure. This theory is based on the fact that the organ is highly sensitive and situated in the fore part of the skull of an animal which dives, head first, sometimes to considerable depths.

Phocaenidae

These are cetaceans with cone-shaped heads and spatulate teeth. The neck bones, three to seven in number, are fused together. In recent years much research has been carried out on the intelligence of these animals.

Class	Mammalia
Order	Cetacea
Family	Phocaenidae

This is the family of the porpoises which have cone-shaped heads without the beak found in many of the species in the same suborder.
They have spatulate teeth and their neck bones, three to seven in number, are fused together. The female's mammary glands open into a single pocket from which the milk is squirted by muscular contraction into the mouth of the calf, which is incapable of sucking. The mother can control these muscles and, therefore, the feeding of her calf.

In porpoises, the weight of the brain in relation to the weight of the body is higher than in any other mammal except man. Besides the large brain, the porpoise has a complex system of communication and the ability to learn and remember.

Common Porpoise

The common porpoise (*Phocaena phocaena*) **averages five feet in length, but some specimens reach six feet.** Weight ranges from 130 to 165 pounds. The head is small, the snout wide and short. The blowhole, which is crescent-shaped, opens on top of the forehead. The body is black on the back, with a green or violet sheen, and white underneath. Teeth vary in number from 94 to 108.

This is a widely distributed species, ranging in the northern hemisphere from the Arctic Ocean to West Africa. It is also found in the North Pacific down to Southern California. It sometimes travels up deep rivers. There is a spring migration to the Baltic, where the animals spend the summer and autumn. Porpoises may be found singly, in couples or in large groups or schools. They are agile, fast swimmers, much given to leaping out of the water. They dive deeply, surfacing to breathe then diving again.

The mating season is in summer, into August. Pregnancy lasts 11 months. The females give birth to one or two calves which are half the length of their mother and weigh about ten pounds. Most calves are born between April and June. The mothers show great affection for their young, defending them courageously and suckling them until they are a year old. Porpoises prey mainly on

(Above)
Like all its relatives, the porpoise has a highly developed brain. It is found in all the seas of the northern hemisphere and sometimes travels up rivers.

fish, especially fish that live in shoals, like herrings, but they also eat squids, crustaceans, and even algae.

Delphinidae

This is the family of the dolphins. They are gregarious animals, found in most of the world's seas. They undertake long migrations, sometimes journeying up rivers.

Class	Mammalia
Order	Cetacea
Suborder	Odontoceti
Family	Delphinidae

This is the family of the dolphins, which are whales with a greatly lengthened snout resembling a pig's. Their length varies from four to 14 feet, and weight ranges from 50 to 500 pounds. Individual animals have been known to reach 30 feet and 1,500 pounds. The blowhole is crescent-shaped with the end pointing forward.

Dolphins are found in almost all the seas of the world. They are gregarious animals which undertake long migrations and sometimes travel up rivers. Man has always been attracted to the dolphin and dolphins have always displayed a certain familiarity with man. Their liveliness, boldness and joyful frolicking have, since time immemorial, attracted sailors and poets.

Almost all dolphins can move at high speed and are extremely agile. This speed and agility makes them formidable predators on fish.

Voracious feeders, they eat mostly fish, molluscs and crustaceans. During the mating season, the males fight fiercely. Pregnancy lasts about ten months. The females give birth to one or two calves which they suckle for a long time.

Pilot Whale

The pilot whale or blackfish *(Globicephala melaena)* **is one of the largest of the toothed whales, sometimes reaching a length of 30 feet. Usual length is about 16 feet and weight about 1,550 pounds.**

The almost spherical head looks grossly swollen. The pectoral fins, which are sickle-shaped, are set low on the flanks; the dorsal fin is situated about the middle of the back. The eyes are at the angle of the mouth—an oblique mouth giving the impression that the animal is always smiling. Each jaw has about 20 long, strong, conical teeth which wear out quickly and are often shed when the animal reaches an advanced age. The skin is hairless, smooth, shiny and uniformly black, except for a gray patch on the throat.

The pilot whale is found in all the seas of the northern hemisphere. In winter, it migrates from the Arctic, often reaching as far south as Gibraltar, and sometimes appearing in the Mediterranean. In summer, it travels north again, often by a different route.

The most gregarious of the whales, it is found in groups of ten to 20, and sometimes in large herds of several hundreds.

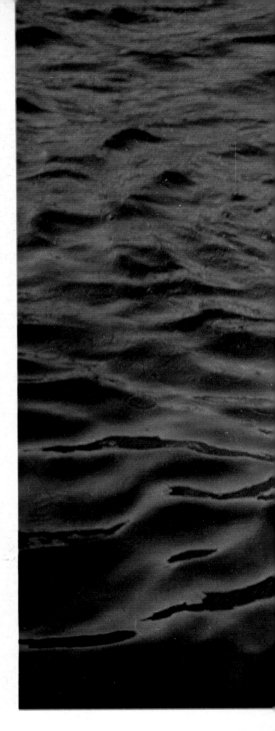

A large herd of blackfish is always headed by an old male: hence the name pilot whale.

They are powerful swimmers, diving and surfacing regularly when on the move. They blow noisily, spouting a jet of air mixed with water about three feet high. When swimming at speed, the head and upper part of the body are clear of the water. When the sea is calm, the herds often rest motionless, with only their heads above water.

This species feeds mainly on squids.

The mating season, in temperate waters, is winter. Pregnancy lasts about a year, and the new born calf measures from eight to nine feet in length. It is suckled for 16 months.

The female pilot whale is sexually mature at three years, by which time it measures 12 feet in length. But the male is not mature until the age of 13 years, when it measures about 16 feet in length. The life span appears to be about 50 years.

Pilot whales are the ones most often found stranded on beaches because their sociable habits make them follow the herd leader blindly, as sheep do. If the leader, during a panic, rushes for shallow water and becomes stranded, the whole herd rushes after it to its death.

The natives of the far north used to kill a lot of pilot whales on migration. Each carcass provided, on average, a ton of oil. Greenland whalers still hunt the pilot whale, killing between 3,000 and 4,000 a year. The flesh is used in the manufacture of composite animal foods, especially dog and cat foods.

Killer Whale

The killer whale, sometimes called the grampus, (Orcinus orca) doesn't usually exceed 16 to 20 feet in length, but some specimens grow to 30 feet. This whale is a savage predator and literature is full of records of its ferocity.

It can be recognized by its large shark-like fin which, in adults, may reach a length of seven feet. The killer is a slender-bodied, extremely strong whale. It has 20 to 24 teeth in each jaw—sharp rending teeth that enable it to tackle prey of great size, including animals larger than itself.

The upper part of the killer whale's body is black, with a few white patches. The

(Left)
Of all cetaceans, pilot whales are the ones most often stranded. When they stray into shallow water, they die, victims of their sheer weight.

(Above)
Pilot whales are gregarious animals that live in large herds, led by an old male—hence their name.

71

under parts are white. There are individual differences in the position of the markings, but the black and the white are always clearly defined. There is always an oval white patch behind each eye. The skin is smooth and shiny.

This whale is found in all the world's oceans, being highly adaptable to changes in water temperature. A sociable animal, it hunts in herds of three to fifty. It usually swims at a speed of six to eight miles per hour. But when it wants to, it can reach the incredible speed of 23 miles per hour. It can make leaps of 40 feet, rising clear of the water to a height of five feet when doing so.

This species can hunt the greatest giants of the sea and is, indisputably, the most voracious and ferocious of all cetaceans, probably of all aquatic animals. Up to 24 seals have been found in the stomach of a killer whale. A male killer whale, measuring 20 feet in length, had 13 porpoises and 14 seals in its stomach. The fifteenth seal had stuck in the killer's throat and suffocated it. Killer whales, in groups of three or four, will even attack the large whales. They will

seize a whale that has already been killed by whalers, fighting among themselves and with the whalers over the carcass. It is also a predator on sea otters, water fowl, fish and squids.

Hunting the killer whale is difficult and unprofitable. As a result, it is little interfered with by man.

Dolphin

The common dolphin (*Delphinus delphis*) **has featured in many fables and legends since ancient times.**
There is the story of Arion who was thrown into the sea by pirates and rescued by dolphins attracted by the sound of his lyre. Then there is the famous story of the boy who, having won the affections of a dolphin, rode on its back in the Bay of Naples. The love uniting boy and dolphin was so great that when the boy died, the dolphin died of grief.
It is recorded that, in antiquity, the dolphin was a servant of man, helping him, for instance, to catch mullet. It won the affection of kings, several of

(Top)
A formidable predator, the killer whale attacks all cetaceans, including right whales. It also eats many seals and sea otters.

(Left)
The killer whale can be recognized by its white under parts and the white patch behind its eye. A fantastic swimmer, it often hunts in herds and can reach a speed of 23 miles per hour.

(Right)
The massive forehead of the sperm whale contains a pocket full of an oily substance, known as spermaceti. This organ may act as a pressure indicator when the animal dives.

whom used it as their emblem on flags and coins. Its strength, intelligence and agility have always attracted man. Roman emperors had a keen interest in all stories about it. The eldest sons of the kings of France were called *Dauphins*.

Dolphins grow to a length of six to eight feet. They have a sickle-shaped dorsal fin, like a shark's, about 25 inches tall. Average weight is about 165 pounds. All dolphins have a prominent beak. The head swells from the base of the neck, and it is most prominent in front of the blowhole. The eyes are situated behind the corners of the mouth, and there is a dark flash leading from eye to snout.

The body is spindle-shaped and thick-set. The skin is smooth, shiny, brownish-green or black on the back, white on the under-side, and is striped with bands of different shades on the flank. The

number of teeth is variable, although there are usually about 200, tiny, pointed and curved slightly toward the inside of the mouth. They are spaced regularly so that the teeth of the upper jaw fit neatly into the spaces between those of the lower jaw.

Dolphins are notable for their habit of following ships. They can stay with a ship that is travelling at 22 miles per hour. They are found in all the warm and temperate seas of the world and sometimes venture into northern waters. Although they prefer to remain in the open seas, they sometimes travel up rivers. The dolphin's back is rigid, so it cannot bend it when it leaps out of the water; it merely lowers its head and tail fin.

A herd of dolphins may number ten to 100 individuals, swimming in two columns. Observers have always been

74

(Top)
The bottle-nosed dolphin has a shorter snout than the common dolphin. It is also bigger. Males sometimes reach a length of 13 feet.

struck by their gregarious and sociable nature. Zoologists have noticed that the members of a herd seem to help each other, so that if one is unable to swim—because of wounds or sickness—the others support it in the water until it recovers or dies.

The teeth of the dolphin indicate the predator. And it is a powerful predator. Yet there is no record of a dolphin attacking man. It eats mostly fish, crabs, squids and other marine animals, but shows a clear preference for fish that live in shoals. Dolphins follow migrating shoals.

Mating takes place at the beginning of the year, and the young are born in late autumn. A female gives birth to a single calf, about 20 inches long, and looks after it with great care and tenderness. It takes ten years for a dolphin to reach maturity and the average life span, formerly believed to be 100 years, does not seem to be more than 30 years.

The greater strength of its tail fin enables the dolphin to leap out of the water. It can bend its head and tail, but its rigid back remains straight.

75

Man's fascination with the dolphin has been reflected in many different ways. Dolphin flesh was once considered a delicacy. Certain parts of its body were used for medicinal purposes. The oil from its liver was used to treat ulcers, and its ashes were used to make various ointments that were held to have miraculous powers.

Nowadays, these wonderful marine mammals have an interest for zoologists, far more important than the taste of their flesh or the miraculous properties of their organs. Research has shown that they have a very high level of intelligence. The trained dolphins in the aquaria of California and Florida have given great pleasure to the public who are attracted by their incredible agility and friendliness. It is now known that dolphins can communicate with each other by uttering audible sounds and a whole range of ultrasonic ones. They hold real conversations with each other —whistling, clicking their tonge, cackling and uttering sharp cries. If a dolphin is in difficulty, it calls out for help. This distress signal is put out intermittently and alerts other nearby dolphins who hurry at once to help.

Recent studies, carried out mainly in the United States, have shown that dolphins are also capable of imitating the human voice. They can learn to laugh, to whistle and, in some cases, even to repeat words. Many experts are now convinced that man will soon be able to communicate with these highly intelligent animals and exchange ideas with them. There is no record of a dolphin ever attacking a man. Indeed, dolphins have already been trained to help man in under-water salvage operations and have taken part in military exercises.

Monodontidae

The cetaceans of this family reach a length of over 13 feet. The neck bones are all separate.	
Class	**Mammalia**
Order	**Cetacea**
Suborder	**Odontoceti**
Family	**Monodontidae**

The animals of this family, when adult, reach a length of over 13 feet. Their skin is lighter than that of other cetaceans, and they can be indentified at once by the absence of a dorsal fin. They have fewer teeth than the other toothed whales and the neck bones are not fused.

Because of their speed, dolphins can easily follow ships. Their sickle-shaped dorsal fin distinguishes them from porpoises.

The legend of the poet Arion, who was saved from pirates by a dolphin, illustrates the respect felt for this cetacean by the Ancient Greeks. Today it is being studied in detail.

This swimmer seems neither surprised nor scared to see a group of dolphins leaping out of the water. This happens frequently around the coasts of Hawaii, were this photograph was taken. The inhabitants of the island trust these friendly beasts of the sea.

Narwhal

The narwhal (Monodon monoceros) is distinguished from all other cetaceans by its teeth. In both sexes there are only two, situated at the front of the upper jaw.

In males, the tooth on the right does not usually break through, while that on the left grows continually, piercing the upper lip and appearing as a tusk winding out anti-clockwise and reaching a length of nine feet. In the females, the teeth grow very little.

Adult narwhals are white or yellowish with irregular dark patches. Young animals are usually dark, but some are white or light gray. The usual length, not including the tusk, is 13 feet, but some narwhals reach a length of 16 feet. The pectoral fins are 12 to 20 inches long; there is no dorsal fin; the tail fin is three to five feet wide.

The strange appearance of this cetacean has always stirred the imagination of man. The tooth of the male was

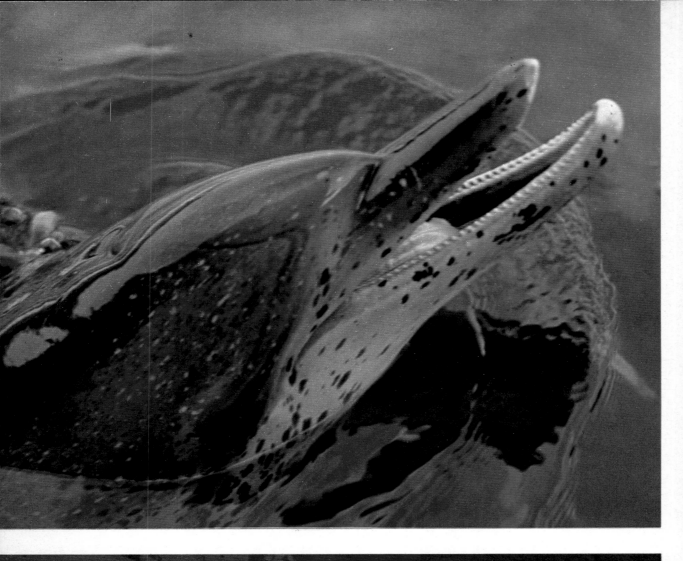

formerly believed to be a horn and was credited with many magic properties, as rhinoceros horn still is in some parts of the world. In the Middle Ages, the narwhal's tooth was thought to be a unicorn horn.

The narwhal is found in the seas of the

(Top, left)
The spotted dolphin lives in the warmest seas. It has a very long beak, and may have up to 200 teeth.

far north, mostly between latitude 70° and 80°, and it rarely ventures south of the Arctic Circle. It lives in small groups of six to ten, often all of one sex. Larger herds form during the southward migration in the autumn and they return northward in the spring. The herds retreat before the advancing ice and return north as it melts.

A very fast swimmer, the narwhal is usually a placid animal, except during the mating season, when the males fight fiercely with their rivals. Males can break their tooth during such fights.

A narwhal calf measures five feet at birth. Single calves are usual.

Narwhals feed on sea slugs, shell-less molluscs, and fish that can be swallowed without chewing. Narwhals' chief enemies are the killer whale and man. They are hunted with a harpoon at

(Left)
The striped dolphin's spermaceti organ extends so far that the beak can hardly be seen. While most dolphins look as if they are smiling, this one's face has a glum expression.

(Above)
Commerson's dolphin, which lives in southern waters, can be recognized by its patches of black and white. Its habits are little known.

airholes in the ice. Narwhals are dependent on these airholes; it sometimes happens that they are trapped under the ice, and they drown if they cannot find a breathing hole.

Beluga or White Whale

The beluga (*Delphin apterus leucas*), **also known as the white whale, is rarely more than 13 feet in length.** The white whale is the better name because the common dolphin is called beluga in Britanny. The great white sturgeon, from which caviar is obtained, is also known as beluga.

At birth, the beluga is black or dark gray, but becomes completely white at the age of four or five years, by which time it weighs 500 to 600 pounds. It has few teeth, a bulging forehead, and a short snout without a beak.

Unlike other cetaceans, it utters sounds under water, but only rarely in open air. It can utter sounds that resemble the sound of a curlew's song in spring—hence its other name of sea canary. It is a sociable animal, usually found in

(*Above*)
The beluga, or white whale, lives in Arctic waters. Dark at birth, it grows lighter with age, and is completely white at four or five years old.

(*Right, top*)
The beluga has a very bulbous forehead and a short snout, without a beak. The strange cries which it emits have earned it the name of "sea canary".

(*Right*)
Unlike most cetaceans, the beluga lives mainly on animals it finds on the sea bed—crabs, worms, fish and crustaceans.

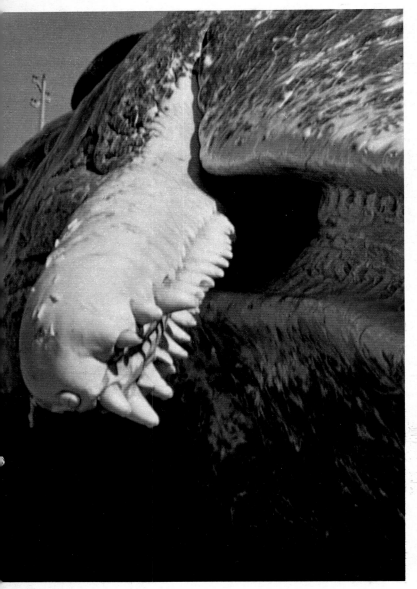

groups of about ten, but sometimes in herds of several hundreds.

The white whale eats literally anything it finds in the sea bed, including fish, crabs, worms and crustaceans, It is not notably migratory, its movements being dictated by the movement of the ice rather than food supply.

Physeteridae

This family has two species—the sperm whale which is 60 feet long, and the pigmy sperm whale which is not more than 13 feet long.

Sperm whales can be recognized by the great box-like head which encloses the greatly developed spermaceti organs. The dorsal fin is absent or very small. The upper jaw is much larger than the lower and the blowhole is situated on the left. Only the lower jaw has functional teeth. Most of the neck bones are fused.

Sperm Whale or Cachalot

The sperm whale (*Physeter catadon*) **is the most bizarre of all cetaceans.**

It is smaller than the great Balaenoptera. The males grow to a length of 50 to 60 feet, and the females up to 36 feet. The enormous box-like head is vertical at the front and is as big as the rest of the body.

The blowhole of the sperm whale is an S-shaped fissure, eight to 12 inches long, situated on the front edge of the snout somewhat to the left. When this whale blows, it spouts at an angle. The small eyes are situated below the angle of the mouth and the ears are below the eyes. The lower jaw is narrower and shorter than the upper which covers it completely when the mouth is closed.

The sperm whale's head and intestines have, literally, been the death of it, because both provide materials used in the cosmetic industry

In the frontal region of the head, there is a large cavity, with a fibrous layer at the bottom filled with spermaceti. This was once highly prized in the manufacture of substances requiring fine, high quality wax. The spermaceti was widely used in cosmetics and medicine and an adult sperm whale can provide almost a ton of this substance.

Apart from the spermaceti, the sperm whale also provides a highly valuable substance known as ambergris, which is produced in the intestines. It looks like wax, has a musky smell, and has the property of fixing perfume. It has been used as a perfume fixative and as a cosmetic since ancient times. Ambergris is passed with the faeces and so can be gathered in small quantities on beaches. But great quantities could be obtained only by killing the whales. So whales were killed. A single sperm whale can provide 1,000 pounds of ambergris from

(Top)
The sperm whale sometimes grows to more than 66 feet. Its enormous head can contain up to a ton of spermaceti, and its intestine contains the substance known as ambergris.

(Left)
The sperm whale's lower jaw, which is much smaller than the upper, is the only one to carry teeth. These fit into the palatal sockets.

its intestines. The market value of ambergris is always high.

The skin of the sperm whale is shiny, hairless, and perfectly smooth. It is black on the back, lighter underneath. These whales are found in all the world's oceans. They are gregarious animals. The males form harems, collecting as many females as they can. As in certain other animals, the patriarch or pasha drives the young males out of the herd, and these young animals sometimes get stranded on beaches. Sometimes several animals are stranded, and this is apparently the result of misinterpretation of echo location signals, due perhaps to the nature of the sea bed in the area.

The sperm whale has a lighter specific gravity than most other cetaceans, and floats when dead. When diving, the animal plunges towards the bottom, head first. The tail fin can be seen sticking up straight out of the water and the whale descends vertically, sometimes to considerable depths. Shoals of cephalopods, and particularly the giant squid, are this whale's favourite food. It hunts them at a depth of 1,000 to 1,200 feet. But the sperm whale is known to be able to dive to a depth of 3,000 feet. Pregnancy lasts from 12 to 16 months. The female usually has a single calf which is 16 feet long at birth and is suckled for at least six months. The maximum life span is not known, but statistics show that males can live for at least 32 years, and females for 22 years.

Ziphiidae

Like the narwhals, this family known as the beaked whales, have only two teeth.

They prey mainly on animals that do not have to be chewed—octopus, squids and cuttlefish, so they don't really need any teeth. The number of functional teeth has been progressively reduced to two.

This family comprises five genera and 14 species. All are now rare, with the exception of the northern bottle-nosed whale.

Northern Bottle-Nosed Whale

The northern bottle-nosed whale (*Hyperoodon ampullatus*) spends the summer in the North Atlantic and is sometimes seen in the Mediterranean in winter.

An adult male will measure 30 feet long, and a female 24 feet. In general appearance, this whale resembles a large dolphin, with a well developed beak and a pronounced spermaceti organ. Young males usually have two teeth in the lower jaw, but older males have only one. Females have two teeth, poorly developed.

The bottle-nosed whale can leap out of the water like a dolphin. When hunting for food, it often dives to great depths, remaining underwater from ten to 20 minutes at a time. It is a gregarious animal that lives in groups of four to 12. If a member of the herd is wounded, the others do not abandon it.

Platanistidae

This family of dolphins is found in fresh water. They are small animals, between six and nine feet in length.

Class	**Mammalia**
Order	**Cetacea**
Suborder	**Odontoceti**
Family	**Platanistidae**

(Top)
The sotalia is a fresh-water dolphin living in the rivers of South America. The natives believe it to be sacred and say it brings back the bodies of drowned men.

(Above)
The northern bottle-nosed whale can reach a length of 30 feet. Its very prominent spermaceti organ can provide up to 220 pounds of spermaceti.

The last family of cetaceans is the Platanistidae. They have the following distinguishing characteristics:

1 A long body with a clearly defined neck.
2 A slender snout.
3 Neck bones not fused.
4 White pectoral fins.
5 A diet composed mainly of fish and small crustaceans.

They live in fresh water—estuaries and rivers.

Amazonian Dolphin

The Amazonian dolphin or Boutu *(Inia geoffrensis)* **has a very slender tapering snout covered with stiff bristles.**

It has 132 to 136 sharp pointed teeth. The slender body, six to 10 feet long, has large pectoral fins. The dorsal fin is very small.

Generally gray, the boutu is more tawny on the back than on the under parts which become lighter with age until they are flesh pink.

The boutu is found in most of the rivers of South America, especially the Amazon and its tributaries and in the Orinoco. It is mostly found singly or in pairs, but small groups of five or six are quite usual.

This species eats small fish, and sometimes fruit that has fallen from trees on to the river banks.

It is active by day and by night, resting intermittently, and surfacing to breathe about every 45 seconds.

The female gives birth to a single calf which stays with its mother until it has reached adult size.

Gangetic Dolphin or Susu

The Gangetic dolphin or susu *(Platanista gangetica)* **is found in Northern India, in the Ganges, Indus and Brahmaputra. It travels upstream as far as there is water deep enough to allow it to swim.**

This dolphin measures between six and ten feet, but there is a record of a female measuring 13 feet. The body is shaped like a long beak. The blowhole is oblong, along the direction of the body. Bony crests, uniting in front of the blowhole, give the head a bulging shape. The tiny degenerate eyes have no crystalline lenses.

This dolphin has 28 or 29 strong, cone-shaped, back-curving teeth on each side of the jaw. The front teeth are longer and finer than the others. The dorsal fin is no more than a fatty flap. It is generally light or dark gray, and paler on the under parts.

Being blind, the Gangetic dolphin has to probe in the mud with its sensitive beak for the small water creatures on which it feeds. It is a completely inoffensive animal, living usually in small groups of three to ten. These groups carry out limited migrations, moving downstream in winter and upstream in summer which is the rainy season.

The gestation period lasts eight or nine months, and calves are born between April and July. A single calf at a birth is the rule. The new born calf, which is 18 inches in length and weighs 15 pounds, spends the first days of its life hanging on by its teeth to one of its mother's pectoral fins.

The flesh of this dolphin is looked upon as a delicacy in several parts of India. Women often eat it because they believe it increases fertility.

Platanistidae are river dolphins with very small dorsal fins. The Amazonian dolphin (top) lives in South America, the Gangetic dolphin (foot) in the rivers of India.